Money Machines

How Algorithms
Are Shaping Finance

By
Thomas Westwood

Money Machines

How Algorithms
Are Shaping Finance

Table of Contents

Introduction

In recent years, the world of finance has undergone a seismic shift. At the heart of this transformation lies artificial intelligence (AI), a technology that has moved rapidly from the realm of science fiction into everyday financial operations. Finance professionals, investors, and tech enthusiasts are witnessing an era where AI is no longer a futuristic concept but a fundamental component already reshaping the financial industry.

This book seeks to explore the dynamic relationship between AI and finance. By unraveling the complexities behind AI's integration into financial systems, we aim to provide a clearer understanding of how this technology is not just improving efficiencies but also fundamentally changing the way financial markets operate. With AI, decisions can be made more quickly, accurately, and strategically, marking a significant departure from traditional financial paradigms.

AI's rise is not an isolated phenomenon but rather a part of a broader technological evolution that includes developments in data science, machine learning, and big data analytics. Finance, an industry traditionally slow to adopt radical changes, now finds itself riding the crest of this technological wave. As financial institutions worldwide harness the capabilities of AI, they're equipped to manage risk better, enhance investment strategies, and even personalize customer interactions, redefining customer service and satisfaction.

The finance sector's embrace of AI also highlights the necessity for professionals in the field to adapt rapidly. This adaptation involves not just understanding and deploying AI tools, but also cultivating a mindset that is open to change and innovation. Knowledge of algorithms, data analysis, and technical proficiency are becoming as indispensable as traditional financial acumen. Thus, this book is intended as a resource for individuals seeking to acquire the skill set needed to thrive in this new paradigm.

Our journey begins with understanding AI's role in finance—how it emerged from a mere curiosity to a game-changing force. From algorithmic trading that executes orders with speed and precision, to robo-advisors delivering financial advice with cost-effectiveness and efficiency, AI's footprint in this industry is vast and varied. As we delve into each chapter, we will explore how AI-driven solutions are crafted, implemented, and optimized to meet the unique demands of the financial world.

Furthermore, we will navigate through compelling case studies showcasing the real-world impacts of AI on financial outcomes. By examining these applications, lessons learned, and the subsequent regulatory and ethical considerations, readers will gain insights into both the power and limitations of AI in finance. Ethical considerations, in particular, are critical as the financial sector grapples with issues of transparency, bias, and fairness in AI systems.

Innovation, of course, brings a host of challenges. Throughout this book, we address concerns surrounding data privacy, cybersecurity threats, and the intricate process of integrating AI into existing financial infrastructures. Financial institutions must strike a balance between embracing cutting-edge technologies and safeguarding sensitive data, a balance that is increasingly vital in today's digital age.

Lastly, we examine the global impact of AI on the financial sector, comparing how different markets have adopted and adapted to these innovations. This aspect highlights the competitive edge that AI can provide, while also pointing to disparities that emerge as countries and corporations vie for technological superiority.

In conclusion, as we set out on this exploration of AI in finance, our goal is to demystify the complex interplay of technology and finance for our readers. Whether you're a finance professional seeking to stay ahead of industry trends, a tech enthusiast curious about AI's tangible applications, or an investor looking to leverage AI for better financial outcomes, this book offers comprehensive insights into the future of finance, framed by the context of technological innovation and human ingenuity.

Chapter 1:
The Rise of AI in Finance

As AI transforms the dynamics of the financial industry, it's reshaping the very framework of how money operates. The rise of AI in finance is not a mere trend but a fundamental shift; it's integrating cutting-edge technologies like machine learning and data analytics into everyday financial processes. This evolution stands to heighten the precision and efficiency with which tasks are performed, from enhancing predictive capabilities in investment strategies to streamlining complex transactions. The finance professionals, tech enthusiasts, and investors who grasp this potent shift will glean insights into the future of finance, redefining how they engage with markets, manage risk, and allocate resources. This chapter offers an exploration into how AI's burgeoning presence is poised to redefine an industry, bringing clarity to the opportunities and challenges that lie ahead.

Understanding AI's Role in Finance

The integration of artificial intelligence (AI) into the financial sector is not just an evolution—it's a revolution, subtly but securely transforming the landscape of finance as we know it. As AI technologies become more ingrained in financial processes, they are reshaping how institutions operate, make decisions, and engage with their clients. In a world where data reigns supreme, AI stands as both a tool and a catalyst, enabling financial institutions to harness vast amounts of information with precision and speed previously unattainable.

AI's foundational role in finance is in its transformative potential to enhance efficiency. By automating routine tasks, AI reduces operational bottlenecks, freeing up human capital for more strategic endeavors. Whether it's through automating customer service via chatbots or managing back-office functions, AI shrinks the time spent on mundane tasks. This shift is not just about saving time—it's also about minimizing errors, as AI systems don't suffer from fatigue or oversight in the way humans might. The reduction of human error has significant implications for industries reliant on precision, such as finance.

Moreover, AI's role is crucial in refining predictive accuracy within the financial domain. Machine learning algorithms sift through historical data to unearth patterns and trends that might escape the human eye. This capability is especially beneficial in portfolio management, where AI can assist in predicting market movements and advising on investment strategies. It's not replacing human insight but complementing it, providing a more robust framework for decision-making that can adapt to evolving market conditions.

Risk management is another area where AI's role cannot be underestimated. Traditional risk assessment models often rely on historical data and fixed algorithms, which may not account for unpredictable variables in real-time. AI, with its ability to analyze diverse data sources—from social media sentiment to geopolitical events—can provide a more comprehensive risk profile. This dynamic approach means that financial institutions can react more swiftly to potential threats, maintaining stability in volatile markets.

A significant benefit AI brings to finance is its ability to personalize customer interaction. In an age where clients expect bespoke experiences tailored to their unique circumstances, AI technologies offer the tools to deliver this at scale. By analyzing customer data, AI systems can recommend products and services tailored to individual financial goals and behaviors. This personalization extends beyond mere product recommendations; it also includes the interaction itself, with AI-enhanced platforms offering client-specific advice and support.

However, the role of AI in finance isn't just limited to enhancing existing processes—it's also about unlocking new opportunities. For instance, AI-powered robo-advisors have democratized investment management, offering low-cost, automated portfolio management services to a broader audience. By lowering entry barriers that traditionally kept smaller investors out, AI is not just changing the financial landscape—it's creating a more inclusive environment for millions of individuals.

The surge in AI's role within finance also introduces complex ethical considerations. The use of AI raises questions about transparency and accountability, particularly when decision-making processes are opaque or misunderstood. As AI systems grow in complexity, ensuring they operate fairly and without bias becomes increasingly crucial. For financial institutions, maintaining trust through ethical AI deployment isn't just a regulatory imperative; it's vital for sustaining consumer confidence and loyalty.

Another critical aspect of understanding AI's role is recognizing its limitations. Despite its capabilities, AI is not infallible. Systems can still propagate biases if the underlying data is flawed, leading to skewed decision-making that may have grave consequences in financial contexts. Addressing these issues involves a continual process of refinement and oversight, ensuring AI models are trained on diverse and representative datasets.

The integration of AI in finance continues to evolve, with new use cases and technologies emerging regularly. As AI systems become more sophisticated, their applications in finance will expand, driven by advances in computing power and data science. The future promises even greater integration, where AI isn't just a tool within finance but a driving force behind innovative business models and services.

Ultimately, understanding AI's role in finance involves acknowledging both its transformative potential and the responsibilities it entails. While it offers unparalleled opportunities for efficiency, risk management, personalization, and inclusivity, it also demands a commitment to ethical practices and continuous improvement. As financial institutions navigate this landscape, they do so with the understanding that AI is a necessary partner in their journey toward modernization and excellence in service delivery.

Evolution of Financial Technologies

The financial industry stands on the shoulders of technological innovations, tracing a fascinating evolution from basic calculators to advanced artificial intelligence systems. The journey hasn't just been about improving computational power; it's been about redefining how we think about and manage money. Let's take a closer look at how the interplay between finance and technology has brought us to this new era dominated by AI.

In the early days, the introduction of the telegraph was revolutionary for financial markets. It facilitated rapid transmission of stock prices across the country, a game-changer for traders who previously relied on slower, more cumbersome methods. This innovation laid the groundwork for the centralization and efficiency that we see in today's markets. It marked the beginning of technology's intertwining with finance, showing what's possible when speed and connectivity are prioritized.

Fast forward a few decades, and we see the emergence of electronic trading systems that began to replace traditional open outcry methods.

Floor traders were gradually sidelined by digital systems capable of executing trades faster than any human. This shift didn't just change the speed of transactions; it transformed entire market structures, opening the door to a more democratized financial market where even individual investors could partake directly via online platforms.

In the 1960s and 1970s, the introduction of mainframe computers further revolutionized the financial industry. These machines allowed financial institutions to store vast amounts of data and perform calculations with unprecedented speed and accuracy. Such technology enabled the automation of many processes, forever changing how banking and investment activities were conducted. Suddenly, the notion that data could drive decision-making gained traction, setting a foundation for what would later become data-driven financial models.

The late 20th century witnessed the rise of the internet, which offered a new dimension of global connectivity. Information started flowing at previously unthinkable speeds. Investors began leveraging real-time data and conducting transactions from anywhere in the world, fundamentally altering traditional investment strategies. The global reach also introduced new challenges, such as ensuring security and privacy on a massive scale.

Entering the 21st century, the advent of mobile technology and smartphones revolutionized personal finance management. Banking apps became ubiquitous, offering consumers a level of control over their finances that required a trip to the bank just years before. The era also saw the birth of fintech companies that disrupted traditional banking models with innovative solutions and increased customer expectations around service and accessibility.

With the explosion of big data and the advent of machine learning, the financial sector began making strides toward more advanced analytical capabilities. The ability to process and analyze enormous datasets became a competitive edge. Banks and investment firms started employing algorithms to predict market trends and make investment decisions, ushering in today's era where algorithms can even drive financial strategies autonomously.

Now, in the age of AI, financial technologies are reaching new pinnacles. AI tools are employed for tasks that range from executing complex trading strategies in milliseconds to personalizing consumer banking experiences using predictive analytics. These advancements have not only increased efficiency but have also introduced profound challenges around regulation, ethics, and the role of human oversight in finance.

One of the most profound shifts observed in recent years is the integration of AI in risk management. Unlike traditional models, which were based on historical data, AI systems use real-time, dynamic inputs to identify and mitigate risks more effectively. This ability to predict and manage risk with higher accuracy is transforming how institutions weigh potential investments and lending decisions, making them more agile and responsive to market changes.

AI's impact isn't confined to financial markets and risk management alone. It's reshaping how we understand and execute credit scoring. Modern AI-driven credit assessment models can analyze more data points than traditional systems, potentially enhancing the accuracy of lending decisions and opening financial services to underserved populations. However, this also brings with it the critical task of ensuring algorithms are free from biases that could lead to discrimination.

As we stand on the brink of even more transformative changes, it's crucial to consider how AI will continue to evolve financial technologies. The potential extends from further enhancing operational efficiencies and reducing costs to offering unprecedented levels of customer service personalization. The impending arrival of quantum computing also promises to elevate the capacities of AI systems, potentially unlocking new frontiers in financial technology.

This evolution of financial technologies showcases a continuous thread of innovation driven by the need for efficiency, speed, and accuracy. As artificial intelligence becomes increasingly central to this narrative, it's reimagining the very frameworks that have governed financial systems for centuries. This evolution not only speaks to the power of technology in transforming industries but also highlights the perpetual need for adaptability and foresight in leveraging these powerful tools.

Chapter 2:
Algorithmic Trading Unveiled

Algorithmic trading isn't just a buzzword in modern finance—it's a fundamental shift that's transforming how markets operate. By automating decisions based on mathematical models and quantitative analysis, algorithmic trading leverages speed and precision unimaginable in traditional settings. Traders now employ sophisticated algorithms to execute orders rapidly, taking advantage of minute discrepancies in market prices. This approach isn't just about eliminating human emotion in trading decisions; it's about utilizing data-driven insights to capitalize on market inefficiencies more effectively. The proliferation of high-frequency trading, a subset of algorithmic trading, highlights the race for computational speed and execution. While the potential for increased efficiency and profitability is clear, it also challenges market stability, necessitating ongoing scrutiny and adaptation. As algorithms dominate financial ecosystems, understanding this evolution becomes crucial for navigating future market landscapes.

Basics of Algorithmic Trading

Algorithmic trading has quietly transformed the landscape of modern finance, marking a shift from traditional broker-driven transactions to machine-executed trades. At its core, algorithmic trading involves the use of specialized software to execute trades based on predefined criteria. This approach significantly enhances the speed and accuracy of trading, allowing investors to capitalize on even minute price differences. With technology's rapid advancement, algorithmic trading has become more accessible, yet mastering its basics requires an understanding of both the technology and the underlying financial principles.

The concept of algorithmic trading is rooted in the fundamental principle of automating the trading process. By using algorithms—sets of rules or instructions—a trader can define the criteria for buying and selling financial instruments. These algorithms consider a variety of factors, such as price, timing, and volume, to make decisions without human intervention. For instance, a simple algorithm might initiate a buy order when a stock's price moves above its 50-day moving average. This automation not only enables faster execution but also reduces the impact of human emotions on trading decisions.

To truly grasp the basics of algorithmic trading, one must appreciate the importance of speed and efficiency. In financial markets, opportunities often arise and vanish in fractions of a second, a window of time where human intervention is practically impossible. Algorithms, however, can analyze vast datasets and execute orders in milliseconds, taking advantage of these brief opportunities. This capability is particularly valuable in fast-paced environments like currency and stock markets, where prices fluctuate rapidly.

Algorithmic trading strategies vary widely, ranging from simple moving average crossovers to complex statistical arbitrage models. One common approach is trend-following, where algorithms are programmed to identify and capitalize on momentum by buying assets that are trending upwards and selling those trending downwards. Another popular method is mean reversion, which posits that prices will revert to their historical average over time. Algorithms designed for mean reversion execute trades when prices deviate significantly from this average, buying low and selling high.

Moreover, algorithmic trading doesn't operate in isolation; it thrives on data. The vast array of data includes historical prices, trading volumes, and even global news sentiment. Algorithms leverage this data to detect patterns and make predictions, a task that would be overwhelming and unfeasible through manual processes. As a result, a key component of successful algorithmic trading is the quality of data and the robustness of the models that process it. Clean, reliable data can be the difference between a profitable strategy and a failing one.

For those venturing into algorithmic trading, it is essential to understand the types of algorithms employed and the markets they serve. Different markets exhibit unique characteristics and volatilities, meaning that a strategy effective in currency markets might not work well in equities. High-frequency trading, a subset of algorithmic trading, focuses on extremely short-term strategies and requires an intricate understanding of market microstructure. Yet, not all algorithmic trading is high-frequency in nature; many traders use algorithms for executing orders efficiently over a longer duration to minimize market impact.

In addition to understanding strategies, aspiring algorithmic traders must familiarize themselves with the risks involved. Algorithmic trading can amplify both gains and losses, making risk management a critical aspect of any trading system. Popular risk management techniques include diversification, position size constraints, and dynamic stops, which automatically adjust based on market volatility. Without effective risk management, even the most sophisticated algorithm could lead to substantial losses.

Further, technology plays a pivotal role in executing algorithmic strategies. The infrastructure supporting algorithmic trading includes powerful computers, high-speed internet connections, and access to trading platforms that provide the necessary market data and order execution capabilities. It's not uncommon for traders to colocate their hardware in data centers near exchanges, reducing latency to critical levels. This infrastructure, while essential, also entails significant costs, influencing the viability of different trading strategies for individual traders and institutional players alike.

Regulatory considerations cannot be overlooked when discussing algorithmic trading. Given its potential impact on market stability, regulatory bodies scrutinize algorithmic practices to prevent manipulative or deceptive behavior. Regulatory frameworks also impose requirements on market participants to ensure fair practices, including the need for algorithms to be thoroughly tested and monitored. Failure to adhere to these regulations can lead to penalties or exclusion from the markets.

Finally, the democratization of technology has opened the doors of algorithmic trading to a broader audience. Thanks to interactive platforms and robust programming languages, even those with limited financial experience can develop and test algorithms. Educational resources and platforms offer scripts and backtesting capabilities, allowing individuals to experiment with various strategies in a simulated environment before committing real capital.

In summary, the basics of algorithmic trading encompass a blend of financial acumen, technological prowess, and strategic risk management. As algorithms increasingly drive financial markets, understanding their foundations is crucial for anyone stepping into the modern finance arena. The interplay of these elements not only unveils the potential of algorithmic trading to enhance performance but also its capacity to reshape the financial industry profoundly.

High-Frequency Trading Explained

High-frequency trading, often abbreviated as HFT, stands at the pinnacle of modern financial markets. It's a domain where microseconds matter and vast volumes of trades traverse global exchanges in the blink of an eye. At its core, HFT leverages advanced algorithms and cutting-edge technology to execute a large number of orders at incredibly fast speeds. It's not just about speed; it's about precision, efficiency, and the strategic intricacies that make HFT a game-changing phenomenon in the world of finance.

The evolution of HFT has roots in the electronic trading systems of the late 20th century, a period marked by the digitization of equity markets and the gradual fading out of traditional floor-based trading. Today, HFT firms are akin to tech giants, employing physicists, engineers, and data scientists to create sophisticated models that exploit minute market inefficiencies. The infrastructure supporting these operations is formidable, encompassing expansive data centers and direct market access to minimize latency.

The strategies employed by high-frequency traders are diverse, ranging from market making and statistical arbitrage to event-driven trading. Market making, for instance, involves providing liquidity to the market by quoting both buy and sell prices. The goal is to profit from the bid-ask spread while maintaining a neutral market position. These strategies require a nuanced understanding of market dynamics and the capability to adapt algorithms in real-time.

One of the pivotal aspects of HFT is its ability to analyze market data at unprecedented speeds. High-frequency traders use a combination of historical data and real-time information to model potential trades. The algorithms are designed to react to specific market signals, executing trades based on pre-set criteria. Each trade is typically small, but the volume over time translates to significant profits. This relentless quest for speed has led firms to employ technologies like field-programmable gate arrays (FPGAs) and colocation services to gain an edge.

Yet, HFT is not without its controversies. Critics contend that it can exacerbate market volatility and lead to scenarios like the "Flash

Crash" of 2010, where stock prices plummeted within minutes. Proponents argue, however, that HFT enhances market liquidity and reduces spreads, ultimately benefiting all market participants. This tension underscores the importance of regulation in managing the impact of high-speed trading on global financial markets.

Regulatory bodies worldwide are constantly examining the implications of HFT on market integrity and transparency. In the United States, the Securities and Exchange Commission (SEC) and the Commodity Futures Trading Commission (CFTC) have introduced measures to oversee and control high-frequency trading practices. These include requirements for real-time reporting and auditing trails, as well as guidelines for firms to follow in the event of market disruptions.

From a technological perspective, the resources dedicated to developing HFT systems are immense. The speed race isn't just about having the fastest algorithms but also about optimizing everything from hardware to network configurations. Firms invest heavily in high-performance computing environments and sophisticated software to remain competitive. Additionally, machine learning and predictive analytics play a growing role in refining trading strategies, allowing systems to better anticipate market movements.

Despite its complexities, understanding the fundamentals of HFT can provide valuable insights into the broader impact of automation in finance. It's a space where financial acumen intersects with technological innovation, pushing the boundaries of what's possible in trading. The learnings from HFT's evolution continue to influence other areas, such as risk management, where speed and accuracy are crucial.

In the future, HFT is poised to grow even more sophisticated, with advances in artificial intelligence driving new capabilities. These developments could enhance the adaptability of high-frequency trading systems, allowing them to process and react to vast quantities of data more intuitively. As the landscape of finance shifts, high-frequency trading will remain a focal point of debate, shaping discussions on ethics, market fairness, and the role of automation in our financial ecosystems.

To summarize, high-frequency trading exemplifies the intersection of finance and technology, encapsulating the rapid pace and high stakes of modern market operations. Its presence will continue to be felt across financial spheres, making it a vital area of study for anyone interested in the transformative power of AI and technology in finance. While challenges remain, particularly around regulation and ethics, the journey of HFT will undoubtedly yield important lessons for the future of trading and market participation.

Chapter 3:
Machine Learning in
Investment Strategies

In the realm of finance, machine learning is revolutionizing how investment strategies are developed and executed. By harnessing vast datasets and sophisticated algorithms, financial institutions are crafting AI-driven strategies that are not only more efficient but also adaptive to market changes. Machine learning empowers investors to identify patterns and predict trends with an accuracy that traditional methods can't match. This dynamic technology transforms raw data into actionable insights, leading to smart investment decisions. As its capabilities expand, machine learning is turning into a staple for asset managers seeking an edge in a competitive marketplace. The implementation of these AI-powered techniques isn't without challenges, particularly in integrating them within existing infrastructures and ensuring robust data governance. Nonetheless, the potential for enhanced returns and decreased volatility makes its exploration an inevitable journey for forward-thinking financial professionals. Embracing this technology promises not just innovation, but a profound shift in how we perceive and act upon financial markets.

Developing AI-Powered Strategies

In the rapidly evolving landscape of finance, developing AI-powered strategies is not just about the integration of technology; it's about leveraging computational intelligence to rethink traditional investment paradigms. At its core, AI-powered investment strategies involve using sophisticated algorithms to analyze market data, identify trends, and make investment decisions that previously required a human touch. While the deployment of algorithms in trading isn't new, the infusion of machine learning methodologies has elevated this practice to uncharted territories, transforming how investment strategies are conceived and executed.

Machine learning, a subset of AI that emphasizes learning from data, offers an unprecedented ability to adapt and improve with each computation. These systems can analyze vast datasets in seconds and find patterns that might be invisible to the human eye. For finance professionals, this capability translates into actionable insights that can optimize portfolio performance, allocate assets more efficiently, and ultimately deliver higher returns. But the shift from traditional analytics to AI necessitates a deep understanding of both the underlying technology and the market environments it seeks to navigate.

One of the significant advantages of AI-powered strategies is their capacity for real-time analysis and decision-making. Whether it's adapting to sudden market shifts or reacting swiftly to news events, AI systems can reassess and adjust strategies on-the-fly. This dynamic approach contrasts sharply with more static, historical analysis-based strategies, which may not keep pace with today's fast-moving markets. The integration of natural language processing, another branch of AI, further enhances these systems by enabling them to evaluate unstructured data, such as social media posts or news articles, thus offering a more comprehensive market sentiment analysis.

But how do these AI systems work in practice? Typically, they begin with robust data gathering from a multitude of sources, ranging from traditional market data feeds to alternative data such as satellite imagery or social media trends. Machine learning models then process this data through various algorithms, such as neural networks or decision trees, to discern patterns or anomalous behaviors. The insights generated inform strategy development by providing predictions on market movements or identifying undervalued assets. These insights are not merely theoretical; they can be directly applied to trading, investment, and risk management practices.

Recent technological advancements have lowered the barriers to implementing AI strategies, even for smaller investment firms. Cloud computing platforms offer scalable infrastructure, allowing these organizations to process massive datasets without investing heavily in physical hardware. Moreover, open-source machine learning libraries and tools, such as TensorFlow and PyTorch, provide the building blocks needed to develop custom AI models, enabling firms to tailor strategies to their specific needs and competitive edge.

However, the promise of AI in investment strategies comes with its own set of challenges. Data quality and integrity stand as pivotal concerns: poor-quality data can lead to inaccurate models, faulty predictions, and misguided strategies. Additionally, algorithmic bias, where a model systematically makes errors because of prejudices in training data, can skew results, leading to ethically questionable investment decisions. Thus, maintaining the integrity of data inputs and being vigilant about biases is crucial for the successful deployment of AI-powered strategies.

Human oversight remains indispensable in this technological transformation. Though AI systems can process and analyze information rapidly, the nuances of financial markets can sometimes elude pure computational logic. Financial professionals play a critical role not only in supervising the output of AI systems but also in applying the contextual knowledge that algorithms may lack. This synergy between machine intelligence and human expertise elevates the entire process, combining computational power with critical thinking and intuition.

In crafting AI-powered strategies, collaboration between data scientists, financial analysts, and technology professionals is vital. This multidisciplinary approach ensures that models are not only technologically robust but also financially relevant and aligned with organizational goals. Tailoring AI technology to the financial domain requires this cross-functional expertise to bridge the gap between raw data and actionable financial insights.

Moreover, transparency and explainability of AI models have become vital components of reliable AI strategy development. Investors and regulators alike demand to know the rationale behind machine-generated decisions. This demand has led to the advent of explainable AI (XAI) techniques, which aim to clarify decision-making processes in otherwise opaque models. By making AI systems more interpretable, finance professionals can build trust with stakeholders and make informed decisions in line with compliance requirements.

Finally, as AI-driven strategies permeate the financial industry, the competitive landscape is likely to shift. Firms adept at integrating AI technologies into their strategies may gain significant advantages, offering superior returns or risk-adjusted performance. However, this also means that others might face obsolescence if they cannot adapt to this new normal. Continuous innovation, ethical use of AI, and a commitment to ongoing learning are essential for maintaining a competitive edge in this AI-driven world.

Developing AI-powered strategies is a journey, one that combines the rigor of financial analysis with the agility of modern technology. As financial markets evolve, so too will the ways AI is employed to craft and hone investment strategies. Embracing this evolution will not only lead to more intelligent investment decisions but will also redefine the roles of finance professionals in an increasingly automated industry.

Case Studies of Successful Implementations

In the evolving landscape of finance, machine learning has made considerable headway, specifically in the realm of investment strategies. This section focuses on significant case studies that showcase how diverse institutions have successfully harnessed the power of machine learning. These implementations highlight not just technological prowess but also strategic acumen in adapting AI-driven models to navigate the complexities of investment decision-making.

One compelling example comes from BlackRock, the world's largest asset manager. They've integrated a machine learning platform known as Aladdin into their investment process. Aladdin combines vast data sets with sophisticated algorithms to offer risk analytics and portfolio management solutions. It provides actionable insights into market trends and asset risks, allowing portfolio managers to make more informed decisions. Aladdin's widespread adoption showcases its ability to enhance decision-making by distilling large volumes of market data into coherent, strategic insights.

Another illustrative case study involves Renaissance Technologies, a pioneer in the field. RenTech, as it is popularly known, operates one of the most successful hedge funds, the Medallion Fund. This fund is renowned for its use of quantitative and machine learning techniques to drive investment decisions. RenTech employs sophisticated algorithms that analyze vast quantities of historical market data to identify profitable trading opportunities. Their approach is a testament to how deeply integrated machine learning can become in crafting dynamic and adaptable trading strategies that respond to real-time market changes.

S&P Global provides another intriguing example. Through its AI-powered Kensho technology, S&P Global offers enhanced data analytics services to investors. Kensho has revolutionized the analysis of financial trends by automating the process of digesting vast and complex sets of data. It scours through historical financial events and market dynamics to provide predictive insights, thus enabling investors to better anticipate future stock performance and sectoral trends. Kensho's predictive capabilities underscore the transformative potential of machine learning in forward-looking financial analysis.

Then, there's the growth witnessed by quant funds that have fully embraced AI. Funds like Bridgewater Associates have built robust models that can process and learn from thousands of economic indicators simultaneously, allowing them to simulate thousands of potential economic scenarios each day. Their adaptive learning algorithms adjust dynamically, offering unprecedented accuracy in macroeconomic forecasting and portfolio adjustment. Such implementation not only optimizes performance but also increases resilience against volatility.

An exciting development also emerges from the realm of robo-advisors. Wealthfront and Betterment have leveraged machine learning to personalize investment strategies for individual clients. These platforms analyze a client's financial situation, goals, and risk tolerance, tailoring advice and portfolio management to optimize long-term outcomes. By continuously learning from market trends and customer behavior, robo-advisors adjust their strategies, ensuring outcomes remain aligned with client expectations and market realities.

A closer look reveals how Goldman Sachs has utilized machine learning for equity trading and investment research as part of their Marcus platform. This platform employs machine learning to extract insights from financial documents and news articles, predicting asset price movements with enhanced accuracy. Goldman's approach illustrates a strategic blend of academic financial theory with real-world data analytics, demonstrating the practical applications of machine learning outside of traditional investment paradigms.

In a different domain, the use of machine learning at JPMorgan Chase for fraud detection and risk management has shown promising results. By training models to identify patterns within transactional data, JPMorgan has significantly enhanced its ability to predict and mitigate potential risks. Their success in this arena highlights machine learning's capabilities beyond direct investment strategies, impacting the broader spectrum of financial safety and reliability.

The success of these case studies boils down to several key factors: data quality, algorithmic innovation, and the ability to merge human intuition with machine-driven insights. Successful firms invest heavily in data infrastructure, ensuring they feed their models with clean, relevant, and diverse data sets. Algorithmic innovation ensures that models remain adaptive and robust, while human oversight provides the final filter for validating strategy alignments with broader financial objectives.

Moreover, these implementations reflect a foundational shift in the cultural mindsets within these organizations. By encouraging a data-driven decision-making culture, firms not only innovate but also mitigate resistance to technologically driven strategies. Adapting organizational structures to incorporate AI and machine learning is not simply a technological challenge but a strategic one that reshapes internal processes and shapes corporate foresight.

Looking forward, these success stories underline the importance of transparency and accountability within AI models. Institutions are increasingly aware of biases that can stem from historical data and are actively implementing measures to ensure their models align ethically with diverse societal needs. This is vital not just for performance but for regulatory compliance and public trust—factors that invariably influence the long-term success of AI-investment strategies.

These case studies merely scratch the surface of what's possible with machine learning in investment strategies, suggesting a future where AI continues to push the boundaries of what's achievable in finance. The lessons learned from these pioneers will not only inspire future innovations but also set a benchmark for how machine learning can be effectively implemented across diverse financial landscapes.

Chapter 4:
Robo-Advisors and
Wealth Management

In recent years, robo-advisors have emerged as formidable players in the world of wealth management, harnessing the power of algorithms to automate investment advice traditionally offered by financial advisors. These AI-driven platforms provide a cost-effective and efficient means for investors to manage their portfolios, offering tailored investment strategies based on individual risk profiles and financial goals. By democratizing access to sophisticated financial planning tools, robo-advisors have broadened the possibilities for individuals to engage in wealth management previously reserved for those with significant assets. Their ability to continuously learn and adapt to dynamic market conditions ensures that investors receive up-to-date, data-driven advice. As financial markets grow increasingly complex, the integration of artificial intelligence into wealth management signifies a pivotal shift, empowering both novice and seasoned investors to navigate their financial futures with greater confidence and precision.

The Emergence of Robo-Advisors

The financial sector, long characterized by personal relationships and trust, has seen a quiet revolution with the rise of robo-advisors. These digital platforms, driven by complex algorithms and data analytics, have redefined how wealth management services are delivered. In an industry traditionally dominated by human advisors, this shift marks a profound change in the landscape of investment management.

Initially, the concept of robo-advisors might have sounded far-fetched. Entrusting an algorithm with personal financial advice seemed too impersonal for many. Yet, with advancements in artificial intelligence and an ever-increasing comfort with digital solutions, these automated advisors have gained traction. By 2020, robo-advisors were managing billions in assets, signaling a significant acceptance among investors seeking efficient and cost-effective alternatives to traditional advisory services.

This transformation can be attributed to several key factors. First, there's the allure of lower fees. Compared to human advisors, whose services often come with substantial costs, robo-advisors provide a more budget-friendly option. They achieve this by leveraging algorithms to automate processes that don't require human intervention, subsequently passing on these cost savings to their users.

Another driving force behind the adoption of robo-advisors is accessibility. Traditionally, wealth management was a service primarily reserved for affluent individuals. However, robo-advisors have democratized access by lowering entry barriers. With minimal account balance requirements, even novice investors can launch their financial journey, benefitting from sophisticated portfolio management tools often reserved for elite clientele.

Critically, robo-advisors embody the trends of personalization through technology. They analyze vast datasets to understand client preferences, risk tolerance, and financial goals, delivering tailored investment strategies. This level of customization was not previously feasible at scale with human advisors, unlocking new potential for personalized service through technology.

As robo-advisors emerged, so too did their capabilities. Early iterations primarily offered portfolio management and diversification, using exchange-traded funds (ETFs) to align with an investor's risk profile and financial aspirations. Today, many robo-advisors include features such as tax-loss harvesting and automatic rebalancing. These advanced functionalities ensure that portfolios remain aligned with the changing market landscape and individual financial objectives.

Moreover, robo-advisors integrate seamlessly into the lives of digital natives. These platforms can be accessed through smartphones and computers, offering easy connectivity and control over investments anytime, anywhere. Coupled with intuitive interfaces and user-friendly experiences, they've attracted a cohort of tech-savvy investors who prefer managing finances at their fingertips.

Despite their growing popularity, robo-advisors do face challenges. One of the primary concerns is the lack of personal interaction. Human advisors bring insights and empathy to financial planning— qualities that algorithms can't replicate effectively. Investors seeking personalized counsel during volatile market conditions or significant life events may find the digital experience lacking in comparison.

Furthermore, robo-advisors depend heavily on data. Ensuring the accuracy and security of this data is paramount, as erroneous inputs can lead to misguided investment decisions. Consequently, data privacy and cybersecurity are vital considerations, requiring robust systems to safeguard sensitive client information.

Another challenge is the potential for algorithmic biases. The reliance on historical data in constructing models can inadvertently perpetuate existing biases, which might affect portfolio decisions. It's critical for developers and financial institutions to remain vigilant in monitoring and refining these algorithms to promote equitable investment outcomes for all users.

Despite these hurdles, the future of robo-advisors looks promising. Their ability to integrate artificial intelligence with financial expertise positions them well in a market that increasingly values efficiency and personalized solutions. As machine learning evolves, these platforms are likely to offer even more refined and nuanced advice, closing the gap between automated and human-powered investment management.

For the finance professional, tech enthusiast, or investor intrigued by the blending of AI with personal finance, robo-advisors represent a compelling case study. They're emblematic of how technology can redefine traditional roles and services in finance, pushing the boundaries of what's possible in wealth management.

In conclusion, robo-advisors have emerged from a niche concept to a formidable force within the investment industry. Their continued evolution is a testament to the power of artificial intelligence to transform the financial landscape, offering both challenges and opportunities as they redefine the rules of wealth management for a digital age.

How Robo-Advisors Benefit Investors

As traditional financial advisory services faced a paradigm shift with the advent of digital technologies, robo-advisors have emerged as transformative tools in wealth management. They represent a confluence of high-end technology and finance, streamlining the investment process through sophisticated algorithms and automation. Leveraging artificial intelligence, these digital platforms offer a host of advantages that are reshaping how investors manage their portfolios.

Robo-advisors democratize access to investment advice, making it available to a wider range of investors. Traditionally, professional financial advice was a privilege reserved for high-net-worth individuals, largely due to the associated costs. Robo-advisors, however, offer lower fees, eliminating the high entry barriers that many investors face. By reducing costs, they make professional-grade investment management accessible to the masses, giving small investors opportunities to optimize their financial growth just like millionaires.

One of the most significant benefits offered by robo-advisors is their capacity for personalized portfolio management. These systems utilize machine learning algorithms that consider an individual's risk tolerance, financial goals, and investment timeline to create tailored recommendations. The personalization of investment strategies meets the individual needs of investors more comprehensively than many traditional advisors, who often rely on more generic approaches due to time constraints or limited resources.

With round-the-clock monitoring, robo-advisors offer unparalleled efficiency and reliability. The markets never sleep, and these algorithms are consistently at work, rebalancing portfolios when necessary to maintain optimal risk levels. This continuous oversight protects investors from market fluctuations and human errors that can lead to financial missteps. The automation of these processes ensures that investment strategies remain aligned with the user's goals without requiring continual human oversight.

Additionally, transparency is a cornerstone of robo-advisors. Through user-friendly platforms, they provide clear insights into investment strategies, fees, and expected outcomes, allowing investors to make informed decisions. This transparency cultivates trust, a crucial factor for investors when choosing a financial service provider. In contrast, traditional models often involve opaque fee structures and complex financial jargon, which can make investors feel sidelined in their own financial planning.

The integration with technology also engenders a unique advantage: data security and privacy. Most robo-advisors implement rigorous security protocols using encryption and other high-tech measures to ensure personal and financial data is protected from breaches. Considering the sensitive nature of financial data, this aspect cannot be overstated, especially in a world where cyber threats are increasingly sophisticated.

Robo-advisors also excel in tax efficiency. They automate tax-loss harvesting, a strategy that minimizes the tax liability by selling securities at a loss to offset gains elsewhere, optimizing the after-tax returns. This function is incredibly advantageous for investors who might not have in-depth tax-related knowledge but wish to leverage every part of their investment legally and effectively.

Despite their numerous benefits, it's important to note that robo-advisors aren't one-size-fits-all solutions. They might not fully replace the human touch element for investors seeking personalized estate planning, retirement advice, or complex tax planning. However, they function as invaluable tools for those with straightforward financial goals and who seek a hands-off approach to investing.

Moreover, robo-advisors play a pivotal role in promoting financial literacy among investors. Through intuitive interfaces and educational resources, they empower users to understand more about financial markets, different asset classes, and the implications of various investment decisions. This educational aspect aids in financial inclusion, fostering an environment where individuals feel more confident and knowledgeable about their financial decisions.

The use of robo-advisors can mitigate emotional decision-making, which often plagues individual investors. Emotional bias has long been recognized as a detrimental factor in investment strategies. By automating the decision-making process, these platforms help prevent investors from making hasty decisions during market volatility, thereby preserving long-term investment potential.

For investors interested in sustainable and socially responsible investing, many robo-advisors offer custom-built portfolios targeting Environmental, Social, and Governance (ESG) criteria. These tailored services allow investors to incorporate their personal values into investment strategies without sacrificing financial returns, appealing to a growing demographic concerned with ethical investment practices.

Finally, the convenience of robo-advisors cannot be overlooked. With access available through mobile apps or web platforms, investors can review and adjust their portfolios anytime and anywhere. This flexibility aligns well with the fast-paced lives of modern investors who demand quick access and instant information.

In summary, robo-advisors provide a plethora of benefits that are redefining the landscape of personal wealth management. Their ability to offer cost-efficient services, personalized financial advice, continuous monitoring, and the use of technology for secure and transparent investing makes them instrumental in shaping the future of investment. As AI continues to advance and evolve, the role of robo-advisors in revolutionizing retirement savings and wealth management strategies will likely expand, making them an indispensable asset for investors at all levels.

Chapter 5:
Risk Management Redefined

In the relentless pace of modern finance, traditional risk management is being reborn through the transformative power of artificial intelligence. As AI takes center stage, it's not just about identifying potential pitfalls; it's about predicting them before they manifest, making the finance industry more resilient than ever. Risk managers are no longer mere gatekeepers but digital pioneers, wielding AI tools that harness vast datasets to foresee challenges and optimize responses. Predictive analytics is becoming the heartbeat of financial strategies, offering a proactive shield against unforeseen market shifts. This evolution isn't just a technological leap; it represents a paradigm shift where swift, data-driven decisions are the norm. As we weave AI deeper into the fabric of financial risk management, we're witnessing the dawn of a smarter, more adaptive approach that rewrites the narrative of risk itself.

AI Tools for Risk Analysis

In the dynamic landscape of modern finance, one area where artificial intelligence (AI) is making substantial waves is risk analysis. Traditionally reliant on human expertise and intuition, risk management is critical for financial institutions, guiding strategies to mitigate potential losses and safeguard investments. With the advent of AI, this process is being redefined, providing a level of precision and foresight that was previously unattainable.

AI tools for risk analysis leverage vast amounts of data to predict and manage financial risks with remarkable efficiency. These tools can analyze historical data and identify patterns that might escape human analysts. By simulating various scenarios and adjusting for numerous variables, AI can anticipate potential risks well before they become apparent to traditional models. This proactive approach gives financial institutions a crucial advantage in minimizing exposure to unexpected events.

One of the primary ways AI enhances risk analysis is through machine learning algorithms. These algorithms can process and learn from massive datasets, continuously improving their predictive capabilities. Unlike static models, which require human intervention to update or reconfigure, machine learning models adapt organically to new information, presenting a flexible solution in a rapidly changing market. The ability to learn and evolve makes them invaluable in detecting nuanced shifts that might indicate rising risks.

Consider the volatility of market dynamics. AI tools can analyze real-time data from multiple sources, including news outlets and social media, using natural language processing (NLP) techniques to gauge market sentiment. This multidimensional approach enriches the analysis, allowing financial organizations to fine-tune their risk management strategies with insights derived from a holistic view of both quantitative and qualitative data.

Moreover, AI-driven systems excel at stress testing. This process involves evaluating how a portfolio would perform under extreme conditions, such as a financial crisis or sudden economic downturn. AI tools can simulate thousands of scenarios with varying parameters, providing financial institutions with a comprehensive understanding of potential vulnerabilities. These insights inform strategic adjustments, reinforcing resilience against unforeseen disruptions.

Risk analysis is not only confined to market risks but also extends to operational and credit risks. In credit risk management, for example, AI can assess the creditworthiness of borrowers with greater accuracy than traditional credit scoring systems. By considering an extensive range of factors, including behavioral data and historical interactions, AI models offer a nuanced assessment that mitigates default risks and optimizes lending decisions.

Furthermore, AI tools enhance compliance and regulatory risk management. Financial institutions face an ever-growing web of regulations designed to safeguard the economy and protect consumers. AI applications can monitor for compliance, identify potential breaches, and ensure adherence to evolving standards, reducing the risk of costly penalties.

While the benefits of AI in risk analysis are significant, they come with challenges. Implementing sophisticated AI systems requires substantial investments in technology and talent. Institutions must ensure data quality and integrity, as flawed data can lead to misguided analyses. Additionally, there is a need for transparency in AI models to maintain trust and avoid "black box" scenarios where decision-making processes are obscured.

The role of AI in risk analysis also demands an evolution in organizational culture. Decision-makers must be open to integrating AI insights into their strategic frameworks, balancing them with human intuition and expertise. This synergy is vital, as AI serves to augment human capabilities rather than replace them entirely.

As AI continues to evolve, its influence on risk management strategies will only intensify, paving the way for more innovative tools and methodologies. Future developments might see the integration of AI with blockchain technologies for enhanced data transparency and security. Such innovations will further refine risk analysis, providing unprecedented levels of precision and trust.

In summary, AI tools are revolutionizing risk analysis in finance by offering deeper insights, predictive accuracy, and unparalleled adaptability. While challenges exist, the potential benefits far outweigh them, aligning with the industry's imperative to stay ahead in an increasingly complex financial landscape. As institutions embrace these tools, they position themselves not just to survive but to thrive amid uncertainty, laying a robust foundation for future growth and stability.

Predictive Analytics in Risk Management

Predictive analytics has evolved into a cornerstone of risk management, offering new dimensions of insight into potential future events. At its core, predictive analytics refers to the use of statistical algorithms, machine learning techniques, and data modeling to analyze historical and current data to forecast future occurrences. It's not only about peering into the future but providing actionable insights that guide decision-making and strategy formulation. This approach transforms risk management from a purely defensive practice into a proactive mechanism, allowing businesses and investors to navigate uncertainties more effectively.

The financial industry has always been fraught with uncertainties and risks. Traditionally, institutions relied on historical data and expert judgment to gauge risks, which often led to conservative estimates and significant human error. Predictive analytics, with its ability to sift through massive datasets, identifies patterns and correlations invisible to the naked eye, offering a more accurate and comprehensive view of potential risks. This shift allows finance professionals to not only anticipate risks but also quantify them with a level of precision unattainable by conventional means.

Consider the insurance industry, which was among the first to embrace predictive analytics in its risk assessment toolkit. Insurers now leverage predictive models to determine the likelihood of claims, calculate premiums, and identify fraudulent activities. By analyzing customer data and external factors such as weather patterns or economic shifts, insurers can adjust their offerings in real time, improving profitability and customer satisfaction. This is a testament to how predictive analytics can enhance operational effectiveness and competitive advantage.

Moreover, the application of predictive analytics is seen vividly in credit risk assessment. Financial institutions use it to evaluate the creditworthiness of potential borrowers more accurately. Traditional methods often led to either granting credit to risky profiles or denying it to worthy applicants due to a lack of nuance in risk assessment. However, predictive models incorporate a diverse set of variables, including non-traditional data like social media activity and online spending habits, to create a holistic profile of the borrower. This functionality not only optimizes credit assessment but also reduces default rates and enables inclusive lending.

Banks and investment firms are harnessing predictive analytics to manage market risks as well. Financial markets are notoriously volatile, with a multitude of factors influencing stock prices, currency exchange rates, and commodity values. Predictive analytics models ingest vast amounts of market data, news, and even geopolitical developments, offering insights into potential price movements and market conditions. Traders and portfolio managers use these insights to make informed decisions, optimizing asset allocation, and hedging strategies to protect against adverse market changes.

The emergence of big data has been a game-changer for predictive analytics in risk management. With the proliferation of digital transactions, social media interactions, and IoT devices, organizations now have access to a wealth of information that can be analyzed for risk evaluation. The challenge lies in effectively harnessing this data.

Tools powered by AI and predictive analytics streamline the process, turning complex datasets into meaningful insights. Organizations that master data utilization stand poised to mitigate risks more effectively, gaining an edge over competitors who lag in digital transformation.

Yet, the transition to predictive analytics is not devoid of challenges. Data quality remains a major hurdle, as predictive models are only as good as the data they are fed. Incomplete, biased, or outdated data can lead to erroneous risk assessments, potentially leading institutions astray. Furthermore, the integration of predictive analytics into existing risk management frameworks demands substantial investments in technology and talent, often a formidable barrier for smaller firms. Thus, mastering predictive analytics demands a strategic balance between technological adoption and robust data governance.

Another significant consideration is the ethical and regulatory implications of predictive analytics. Financial institutions must navigate the landscape with a keen eye on data privacy and legal compliance. As predictive models often involve processing personal data, ensuring adherence to regulations like GDPR or CCPA is paramount. The potential for algorithmic bias is another ethical concern, necessitating transparency and fairness in model design and deployment. As financial AI evolves, so too do the regulatory frameworks, which demands constant vigilance and adaptation from institutions.

Looking ahead, the potential for predictive analytics in risk management continues to expand. As AI technologies become even more sophisticated and the volume of data grows, we can expect predictive models to become more nuanced and precise. The advent of real-time data processing, advances in machine learning algorithms, and the integration of different data sources promise a brighter future for predictive risk management. Organizations that invest in predictive analytics today will not only better manage current risks but also position themselves strategically for the unpredictable challenges of tomorrow.

In summary, predictive analytics is redefining risk management by converting uncertainty into opportunity. Its ability to analyze vast quantities of data and uncover hidden patterns allows businesses to anticipate future risks with unprecedented accuracy. As financial institutions embrace these technologies, they can move beyond reactive risk management to a forward-looking approach, crafting strategies that anticipate changes and seize opportunities as they arise. In an industry where the only constant is change, the strategic implementation of predictive analytics could well become the differentiator between the leaders and the laggards of tomorrow's financial realm.

Chapter 6:
Natural Language
Processing in Finance

Natural Language Processing (NLP) has gained a significant foothold in the realm of finance, transforming how professionals interact with data and derive insights. In an industry where timely and informed decisions are paramount, NLP applications are proving indispensable. By analyzing vast amounts of textual data, such as news articles, earnings transcripts, and social media feeds, financial professionals can gauge market sentiment and predict price movements with increased accuracy. NLP techniques are also being applied to investment research, enabling a more nuanced understanding of market trends and potential risks. This capacity to decipher and quantify unstructured data is redefining traditional paradigms, introducing a level of analytical depth that was previously unimaginable. The integration of NLP in the financial sector is not just a technological enhancement but a strategic necessity, providing competitive edges and inspiring innovative approaches to investment and risk management. As these technologies evolve, their impact on the financial landscape will continue to expand, opening new avenues for growth and efficiency.

Sentiment Analysis for Financial Markets

In the complex landscape of financial markets, sentiment analysis has emerged as an influential tool, providing invaluable insights that drive investment decisions. As we continue to witness the integration of Natural Language Processing (NLP) within finance, understanding public mood becomes essential for traders, investors, and financial analysts. By examining the collective mood extracted from news articles, social media, and financial reports, sentiment analysis offers a window into the emotional landscape of the market participants. This can be a powerful predictor of market movements, influencing trading strategies and decisions.

In essence, sentiment analysis operates at the intersection of language processing and financial forecasting. It involves the process of analyzing text to determine the writer's attitude or emotional tone. Financial sentiment analysis utilizes various sophisticated algorithms to process unstructured data and identify whether the information is positive, negative, or neutral. This insight allows financial professionals to anticipate market reactions more accurately, thus crafting more informed strategies. The ability to gauge the emotional tone of market reports or public sentiment on platforms like Twitter provides a competitive edge that traditional financial analyses might overlook.

The roots of sentiment analysis in finance can be traced back to behavioral economics, where investor psychology is understood to play a critical role in market dynamics. Opinions, beliefs, and attitudes can influence asset prices even in the absence of fundamental changes. Algorithms now help quantify these qualitative aspects from a vast corpus of available data, often in real-time. This shift from intuition-driven decisions to data-centric strategies marks a significant evolution in market analysis and reflects the broader trend of data-driven decision-making powered by advancements in AI.

Technological advancements in NLP have propelled sentiment analysis to the forefront of financial innovation. Early iterations relied on basic keyword matching and simple sentiment dictionaries. However, the modern approach has evolved significantly, thanks to machine learning models capable of understanding contextual nuances and complexities in human language. These models learn from millions of data points, refining their understanding of linguistic subtleties and domain-specific terminologies. Consequently, sentiment analysis tools today offer financial analysts deeper insights into the market psyche, often uncovering patterns that are not immediately obvious.

Among the prominent applications of sentiment analysis in finance is the prediction of stock price movements. By scrutinizing investor sentiment gleaned from news and social media, analysts can forecast potential price directions. Studies have demonstrated that spikes in negative sentiment can presage downturns, while positive sentiment often correlates with price increases. For instance, a flurry of pessimistic tweets regarding a company might prompt a sell-off, highlighting the media's role in shaping market sentiment. These real-time analyses enable traders to make proactive rather than reactive decisions.

Incorporating sentiment analysis into trading algorithms has become commonplace. Quantitative analysts, often known as quants, integrate sentiment scores into their trading models to enhance the predictive accuracy. These models factor in not just current sentiment but also historical sentiment trends, enabling a more comprehensive analysis. By juxtaposing sentiment with traditional indicators like moving averages or RSI, traders can develop more robust prediction models. The layering of sentiment data, with price and volume data, increases the dimensionality of analyses, offering a more holistic view of market dynamics.

For institutional investors, sentiment analysis provides strategic advantages as well. Asset managers leverage sentiment analysis to manage risks and deploy capital more efficiently. By assessing the public mood and media narratives, managers can identify emerging risks, opportunities, and potential sectoral shifts before they materialize in market fundamentals. By understanding how mainstream narratives can impact investor behavior, asset managers can position themselves advantageously, gaining first-mover advantages in rapidly changing markets.

The rise of sentiment analysis has also fostered the development of specialized financial platforms and tools. These technologies aggregate vast amounts of online textual data and deliver sentiment-based insights in real-time. Tools like Bloomberg's Sentiment Analysis application, or platforms such as Reuter's Eikon, empower users with comprehensive sentiment metrics directly integrated into their dashboards. For retail investors, these insights have democratized access to information previously reserved for institutional analysts, democratizing the playing field.

Despite its advantages, sentiment analysis isn't without challenges. Noise in data, the effects of fake news, and the dynamic nature of language remain significant hurdles. Machine learning models, while advanced, must constantly adapt to new linguistic constructs, cultural variations, and evolving idiomatic expressions. Moreover, distinguishing genuine sentiment from venture-funded hype or coordinated misinformation campaigns can be challenging. Thus, ensuring the continual refinement of sentiment models remains a priority for financial technologists.

Moreover, ethical considerations loom large. The use of sentiment analysis raises questions about data privacy, algorithmic transparency, and the potential for market manipulation. Regulations are echoing these concerns, emphasizing the need for responsible AI deployment. There's a fine balance between harnessing sentiment insights and ensuring these technologies are used ethically and within the framework of financial regulations.

In conclusion, sentiment analysis stands as a testament to the transformative power of AI in finance. As markets continue to evolve, the ability to dissect, understand, and capitalize on sentiment will likely grow in importance. Integrating these insights with comprehensive AI strategies positions financial professionals at the cutting edge of market intelligence. Looking forward, the convergence of sentiment analysis with emerging technologies like deep learning and blockchain promises to unlock new dimensions of market analysis. With ongoing advancements, sentiment analysis will undoubtedly become more sophisticated, offering unprecedented opportunities for those who harness its full potential.

NLP Applications in Investment Research

Natural Language Processing (NLP) has transformed the way investment research is conducted. It's a tool that financial professionals are now leveraging to gain insights from vast amounts of unstructured data, such as news articles, earnings calls, and social media feeds. With the explosion of information available today, NLP serves as a crucial mechanism to sift through data and extract actionable intelligence. This chapter delves into the various applications of NLP within investment research, providing a closer examination of its impact on efficiency, accuracy, and decision-making.

One of the primary applications of NLP in investment research is sentiment analysis. This technique evaluates the sentiment behind spoken or written language to understand investor mood and predict market movements. For example, when a company's earnings report is released, NLP algorithms can quickly analyze the report's text alongside media commentary to assess market sentiment. This real-time sentiment analysis offers investors a competitive edge, enabling them to act swiftly on potentially market-moving information.

Beyond sentiment analysis, NLP is used to perform event detection, which identifies significant events that might impact stock prices. By scouring news articles, social media, and various publications, NLP algorithms can pinpoint events like mergers, acquisitions, regulatory changes, or technological advancements. Investors who capitalize on these insights can adjust their portfolios proactively, rather than reacting after the fact.

Moreover, NLP automates the analysis of earnings calls and investor presentations. Traditionally, analysts would spend hours sifting through transcripts to identify key pieces of information. With NLP, this task is expedited with automated scripts that highlight important metrics, sentiment shifts, and recurring themes. This allows analysts to focus on deeper analysis and strategy rather than the tedious task of data extraction.

In addition to processing textual data, NLP helps investors perform due diligence more thoroughly. Companies are increasingly transparent with their operations, announcing changes or updates across multiple platforms. NLP algorithms compile and synthesize this information, providing investors with a comprehensive overview of a company's performance and risks. This capability is particularly beneficial for portfolio managers who need to assess numerous companies on a regular basis.

Risk monitoring and management also benefit from NLP applications. By analyzing narratives across financial news and reports, NLP can identify potential risk factors that might not be immediately obvious. Whether these risks pertain to geopolitical events, commodity fluctuations, or regulatory changes, NLP enables investors to stay informed and prepared for uncertainty. This proactive risk management tool ensures that portfolios are not exposed to unforeseen threats.

NLP's integration in investment research extends to thematic investing, where algorithms identify and analyze major themes such as sustainability, technological innovation, or demographic shifts. By recognizing these trends from text data, NLP supports the creation of theme-based investment strategies that align with macroeconomic changes. Investors can thus position themselves advantageously by understanding these broader market forces.

Another innovative use of NLP is in the automation of investment reports. Generated reports are often voluminous and riddled with jargon, making it tough for stakeholders to distill essential points quickly. NLP algorithms synthesize and distill these reports into digestible summaries, saving time for investors while ensuring that no critical information is lost. This ability to generate concise and informative summaries is invaluable in rapid decision-making environments.

Furthermore, NLP can enhance collaboration between human analysts and AI systems. By facilitating the interaction between machine analyses and human intuition, NLP fosters a novel environment where symbiotic relationships can develop. Machines offer speed and pattern recognition, while humans contribute contextual understanding and creativity. This collaboration leads to richer insights and more robust investment strategies.

In an era where the ability to process and understand data at scale is becoming a requisite, NLP stands out as an enabler for cutting-edge research in finance. Its applications go beyond merely parsing text; NLP is shaping the future roles of financial analysts by empowering them to leverage data that was previously too unwieldy to manage effectively. As NLP technologies continue to evolve, their integration into investment research will deepen, reaching new dimensions of complexity and capability.

As NLP continues to advance, it will likely incorporate more sophisticated techniques like deep learning to enhance its capabilities. Future NLP applications might exploit these techniques to better capture nuances in language and context, which are notoriously difficult for algorithms to interpret. With ongoing improvements, NLP is set to transform not just how investment research is conducted but how insights are generated and consumed across the financial sector.

In conclusion, NLP has become an indispensable asset in investment research, offering tools that help decode thousands of pieces of new information arriving every day. From interpreting sentiment to detecting key events, to automating reports, its applications are varied and impactful. As the technology continues to mature, it promises to usher in even more sophisticated methods of understanding complex financial landscapes, greatly enhancing the abilities of investment professionals to keep pace in an increasingly fast-moving world.

Chapter 7:
AI and Credit Scoring

In the realm of credit scoring, artificial intelligence is carving out new pathways by fundamentally altering how lenders assess creditworthiness. Traditional methods relied heavily on static data and conventional scoring models, which often failed to capture the complete financial picture of an individual. With AI, however, vast data sets, including alternative data sources like social media behavior and digital payment patterns, are being harnessed to create more nuanced and dynamic credit profiles. This transformative approach not only enhances predictive accuracy but also opens the door for financial inclusion by considering non-traditional credit factors. Yet, as AI systems increasingly shape credit decisions, they also introduce the challenge of eliminating inherent biases that could arise from historical data patterns. The quest to reduce bias in AI-driven credit assessments showcases both the potential of technology to make fairer lending decisions and the imperative for careful oversight to ensure transparency and accountability in the financial sector.

Innovations in Credit Assessment

The financial landscape is undergoing a seismic shift with the integration of artificial intelligence, particularly in credit assessment. Traditional credit scoring models often rely on static parameters like credit history, income stability, and existing loans. While these methods have served well in the past, they aren't wholly reflective of an individual's true creditworthiness, often leaving unbanked populations and startups in the dark. AI has emerged as a transformative force, enabling a more holistic and dynamic approach to credit assessment.

One of the most significant innovations AI brings to credit assessment is its capability to analyze a diverse set of data points beyond the conventional credit report. AI systems can assess alternative data, including online behavior, social media activity, transaction history, and even smartphone usage patterns. This integration of disparate data sets allows for a more nuanced risk assessment process. For instance, an individual without a substantial credit history, such as a young adult or immigrant, might still be able to demonstrate financial reliability through consistent bill payments or responsible social media interactions. By analyzing these alternative metrics, AI systems enable credit issuers to expand their reach to underserved markets.

Moreover, machine learning algorithms have become the backbone of predictive credit scoring models, processing vast quantities of data to identify patterns and trends. These algorithms can predict default risk with greater accuracy than traditional models by continuously learning from new data. This adaptability not only enhances the precision of credit assessments but also supports dynamic credit scoring—a real-time evaluation of a borrower's financial health. Banks and financial institutions can adjust interest rates or credit limits as a customer's economic situation changes, providing a tailored customer experience that improves satisfaction and minimizes risk.

Artificial intelligence is also facilitating the rapid processing and evaluation of credit applications. In the past, assessing a loan application could take days, if not weeks. With AI systems, this process is now nearly instantaneous. Natural language processing (NLP), a subset of AI, plays a pivotal role here. By automating the review of application documents, NLP systems can extract essential information and flag potential issues, all while reducing human errors and biases inherent in manual evaluations. This efficiency not only speeds up the decision-making process but also cuts operational costs for financial institutions.

Fraud detection has reached unprecedented levels of sophistication with the introduction of AI in credit assessment. Machine learning algorithms scrutinize transaction patterns, identifying anomalies that could signify fraudulent activities. These systems are so robust that they adapt to emerging fraudulent techniques, maintaining an up-to-date defense mechanism. Consequently, financial institutions are better equipped to protect themselves and their clients from potentially devastating financial crimes.

AI-driven credit assessment platforms are also enhanced by their capacity to reduce biases traditionally associated with lending decisions. Many conventional credit models inadvertently perpetuate discrimination due to the inherent biases in the data sets they rely on. AI's ability to incorporate a wide range of data sources allows for a more balanced assessment. Additionally, the transparency of AI systems offers an added layer of accountability. While it's true that AI can still reflect biases present in its underlying data, continuous monitoring and refinement of these models can mitigate such issues.

Blockchain technology is complementing AI innovations in credit assessment. Combining these two technologies results in a more secure and transparent system. Blockchain can ensure the integrity of data used in credit assessments, providing an immutable audit trail that enhances trust between lenders and borrowers. This synergy not only paves the way for more secure lending processes but also boosts consumer confidence by offering a clear view of how their creditworthiness is determined.

Several fintech startups are leading the charge in AI-driven credit innovation. These companies often operate with more agility than their larger counterparts, allowing them to implement and iterate on AI technologies quickly. Startups are crafting bespoke solutions leveraging AI to better serve niche markets, such as small businesses or gig economy workers, who frequently lack access to traditional credit avenues. By providing tailored products that better reflect these groups' financial realities, these companies are redefining what is considered creditworthy.

While AI has undoubtedly reshaped credit assessment, it's crucial to address the ethical considerations of these innovations. Privacy concerns arise from the extensive use of personal data, and there needs to be a delicate balance between innovation and consumer rights. Financial institutions must ensure transparency in how AI models are being used to evaluate creditworthiness and put safeguards in place to protect sensitive information.

Collaboration between AI developers, credit institutions, and regulators is essential for realizing the full potential of AI innovations in credit assessment. Regulatory bodies must be proactive in establishing frameworks that encourage innovation while safeguarding consumer interests. Open dialogues and partnerships can foster a conducive environment for advancing AI credit assessment technologies responsibly.

In conclusion, AI is revolutionizing credit assessment by providing more accurate, fair, and efficient evaluations. The continuous evolution of AI technologies promises ongoing enhancements in understanding and evaluating credit risk, ultimately leading to greater financial inclusion and better-served consumers. As these innovations continue to unfold, they will undoubtedly redefine the future of credit and lending, making them more responsive to the needs and realities of the 21st-century economy.

Reducing Bias in Credit Decisions

AI's integration into credit scoring has promised enhanced accuracy and efficiency in evaluating creditworthiness. Yet, it's not without its challenges, particularly concerning the perpetuation of bias. Credit decisions historically suffer from discriminatory practices rooted in flawed data. AI systems, if not carefully managed, can unintentionally replicate these biases, leading to unfair credit evaluations. This section delves into understanding how biases manifest in AI-driven credit scoring and explores strategies to mitigate these biases effectively.

The root of bias in AI credit scoring often begins with the data. Credit models learn from historical data which can reflect societal biases or institutional prejudices. For instance, certain demographics might be underrepresented in credit datasets, making AI systems less accurate in assessing their creditworthiness. If an AI algorithm is trained on such skewed data, it risks making biased predictions. It doesn't inherently understand fairness—its decisions are as impartial or prejudiced as the data it ingests.

Addressing this bias requires both technological interventions and a commitment to ethical practices in data management. One of the primary methods involves diversifying the training datasets. Incorporating diverse data points helps create a more balanced machine learning model. Including variables previously overlooked, like alternative credit data sources—think rental and utility payments—can provide a fuller picture of an individual's financial behavior.

In addition, feature selection plays a critical role in shaping an AI model's fairness. By analyzing and choosing features that do not correlate with prohibited factors such as race or gender, developers can curb potential bias. However, these factors often indirectly influence credit decisions through proxies, such as zip codes or professions.

Identifying and minimizing the use of proxy features helps in building models that do not inadvertently discriminate.

Moreover, transparency in AI systems can significantly contribute to reducing bias. Explainable AI (XAI) is pivotal here. It involves creating models that allow stakeholders to understand and interpret the decision-making process. By exposing the underlying mechanics of an AI model, it becomes easier to detect and address bias. Financial institutions are adopting XAI to ensure that their AI systems align with regulatory standards and ethical expectations.

Implementing fairness-aware machine learning algorithms is another strategy. These algorithms are specifically designed to account for fairness constraints, adjusting their learning processes to reduce disparate impacts on different groups. Techniques like reweighting training data or adjusting decision thresholds allow these models to make more equitable decisions.

While technical solutions are vital, reducing bias in credit decisions fundamentally requires a cultural shift within financial institutions. There's a growing recognition of the need for multidisciplinary teams comprising ethicists, sociologists, and domain experts alongside data scientists and engineers. Diverse teams bring varied perspectives, ensuring that AI solutions consider a broad spectrum of factors influencing fairness.

Critical assessments of AI models via regular audits also bolster bias reduction efforts. Routine checks help identify patterns that suggest bias, enabling timely interventions. Audits can be both internal and external, adding layers of scrutiny to validate that AI systems uphold ethical standards.

Several financial institutions are actively testing bias mitigation strategies. For example, they've launched pilot programs addressing credit assessment practices and proactively adjusted lending criteria to factor in bias reduction. Collaboration between regulators and financial institutions is also paramount. By working together, they can establish guidelines and incentives that encourage the development and deployment of fair AI systems.

Bias in credit decisions not only raises ethical concerns but also presents inherent risks to business sustainability. AI systems perceived as biased can erode customer trust and lead to reputational damage. On the flip side, committing to fairness can enhance brand reputation and expand customer bases, offering a strategic advantage in competitive markets.

Mitigating bias does not imply compromising on accuracy or business objectives. It's about achieving a balanced approach where AI systems not only perform optimally but also uphold fairness. This blend of responsibility and innovation ultimately leads to a financial ecosystem that champions equity, serving diverse communities equitably.

In conclusion, reducing bias in AI-driven credit decisions is a multi-faceted challenge requiring ongoing vigilance and adaptation. The solutions are dynamic, involving data integrity, algorithmic transparency, and regulatory engagement. As financial institutions pave the way with responsible AI implementations, they also set a precedent for broader applications across various sectors. This endeavor isn't just about leveraging technology; it's about shaping a future where financial fairness and innovation coalesce.

Chapter 8:
Blockchain and AI

The fusion of blockchain and AI heralds a new era in the financial sector, promising to enhance both security and efficiency. These two cutting-edge technologies converge to offer decentralized solutions and powerful data analytics, transforming traditional financial processes. Blockchain provides a tamper-proof ledger, ensuring transparency and accountability, while AI's learning algorithms extract insights from vast datasets. Together, they streamline operations such as fraud detection and transaction verification, enabling quicker and more reliable financial services. As these technologies continue to evolve and intertwine, they foster innovation, offering finance professionals a toolkit to address complex challenges, reduce costs, and drive intelligent decision-making. By leveraging the strengths of both blockchain and AI, the finance industry is poised for a future where technological sophistication meets pragmatic applications.

The Intersection of Blockchain and AI

The intersection of blockchain technology and artificial intelligence is more than just a convergence of two buzzwords. It's a potent blend, promising to reshape financial systems, enhance transparency, and unlock unprecedented efficiencies. As the financial world increasingly leans on advanced technologies, understanding how these two transformative forces interact is crucial. Blockchain and AI, each revolutionary in their own right, together unfold new possibilities that neither could achieve alone.

Blockchain, by design, offers a decentralized, immutable ledger of transactions. It's the backbone of cryptocurrencies like Bitcoin and Ethereum, but its applications extend far beyond. On the other side, AI stands as a tool for decision-making that can analyze vast quantities of data, identify patterns, and offer insights with remarkable accuracy. When these two technologies merge, they can address fundamental challenges existing in siloed financial systems.

AI's strength lies in its ability to process and learn from data. However, the effectiveness of AI depends on the quality and reliability of the data it uses. Blockchain technology provides a secure, verifiable base for data integrity, ensuring that AI models work with trustworthy inputs. This combination can be particularly transformative in areas where data tampering is a significant concern, such as regulatory compliance and audit processes.

For example, consider the process of Know Your Customer (KYC) compliance. KYC mandates financial institutions to verify the identity of their clients, a task that's traditionally time-consuming and fraught with potential for human error. AI tools, backed by an immutable blockchain record, can automate identification processes, making them faster and more reliable while significantly reducing costs and security risks associated with data breaches.

Furthermore, the integration of AI in blockchain environments offers a way to enhance the interpretability and utility of blockchain data. Financial professionals can use AI to parse through blockchain's vast ledgers, identifying patterns and predictive analytics that can inform investment strategies and risk assessments. This is a significant leap forward, considering how difficult it can be to extract actionable insights from raw blockchain data manually.

When applied to smart contracts, the intersection of AI and blockchain becomes even more pronounced. Smart contracts—self-executing contracts with terms directly written into code—are vital in automating and enforcing agreements across platforms. AI can augment these contracts by predicting potential disputes or failures in the contract execution stage, prompting interventions before issues escalate. This predictive capability enhances the reliability and functional utility of smart contracts, paving the way for more complex financial transactions.

In the realm of asset management, AI-powered algorithms utilizing blockchain-secured data can perform real-time analytics and execute trades with little human intervention. This auto-executive capability allows for high-frequency trading systems that not only react to market changes instantaneously but also do so in a secure, tamper-proof environment provided by blockchain. It promotes fairness and transparency, reducing fraudulent activities that could otherwise go unchecked.

Decentralized finance (DeFi) exemplifies the potential of blockchain and AI in transforming traditional banking systems. DeFi platforms operate without traditional intermediaries, allowing borrowers, lenders, and investors to interact directly via the blockchain. AI algorithms can effectively manage the risk assessments on these platforms, ensuring robust, decentralized financial services without the need for centralized authorities.

Yet, this integration isn't without challenges. One significant hurdle lies in the computational resources required. Blockchain networks are often criticized for high energy consumption and latency issues. Pairing these with AI's demanding computational needs could exacerbate these issues, potentially leading to scalability concerns. Therefore, optimizing AI models to work within blockchain's constraints without compromising efficiency is critical.

Thomas Westwood

Interoperability is another challenge. For blockchain and AI to work cohesively, data protocols and standards must be established to facilitate seamless interactions between independent systems. This requires collaboration across various sectors and agreements on data standards, which can be challenging given the decentralized nature of both technologies.

Furthermore, privacy concerns around AI and blockchain integrations can't be ignored. Blockchain's transparency, though a strength, can conflict with privacy needs, as all data on a blockchain is open for viewing by default. Finding a balance between transparency and privacy, perhaps through new cryptographic techniques like zero-knowledge proofs, is crucial for broader adoption in sensitive financial applications.

Despite these challenges, the financial industry is witnessing growing enthusiasm for AI and blockchain collaborations. Startups and established financial institutions alike are experimenting with pilot projects that test the waters of this intersection. Early successes in this domain highlight the potential for significant cost savings, enhanced security protocols, and improved service delivery in financial systems.

Conclusively, the fusion of blockchain and AI marks the beginning of a new era in finance. It's an era characterized by increased efficiencies, deeper insights, and an enhanced trust framework. As these technologies mature and overcome their growing pains, they hold the promise of not only disrupting but also improving the fundamental mechanisms of global finance, opening the door to a multitude of new opportunities and innovations. Financial professionals and investors keen on staying ahead of the curve must keenly study and anticipate the implications of this transformative convergence. The journey may be complex, but the potential rewards for those who navigate it correctly are immense.

Enhancing Security and Efficiency

The confluence of blockchain and AI represents a tectonic shift in the landscape of financial systems, ushering in a new era of security and efficiency. Blockchain, with its decentralized ledger technology, offers unparalleled transparency and immutability, while AI's analytical prowess introduces enhanced predictive capacities and automation. Together, they fortify the financial sector against inefficiencies and cyber threats, addressing some of the industry's most persistent challenges.

At the heart of this transformation is the concept of decentralization. Traditional systems rely heavily on centralized authority, which can be both a strength and a vulnerability. By contrast, blockchain distributes data across a network, reducing single points of failure and increasing resilience. When AI is layered on top of these distributed systems, it can swiftly analyze and predict potential weaknesses or fraud patterns, leading to stronger defense mechanisms.

The synergy between blockchain and AI is particularly evident in enhancing transactional efficiency. Financial transactions, especially cross-border ones, often involve numerous intermediaries which slow down the process and add to costs. Blockchain's ability to provide a single, verifiable source of truth can streamline these transactions. AI can further optimize this process by predicting transaction times, and calculating costs based on real-time data, thereby diminishing delays and lowering fees.

Moreover, blockchain's transparency is a powerful asset in fostering trust among stakeholders. Every transaction is recorded in an immutable ledger, which is accessible to all participants in the network. This level of transparency is complemented by AI's ability to conduct real-time audits and assessments. Such audits are not only comprehensive but also immediate, reducing the need for extensive manual oversight and thereby cutting operational costs.

Fraud detection stands to benefit enormously from the tandem use of AI and blockchain. Financial fraud, which costs the global economy trillions annually, thrives in opaque systems. Blockchain's transparency allows for clear traceability of transactions, making it easier to spot anomalies. AI systems, trained on vast datasets, can identify these anomalies quickly and efficiently, potentially halting fraudulent activities before significant losses occur.

Consider smart contracts, which are programmable agreements that automatically execute the terms written into code. They are a natural melding of blockchain and AI, ensuring that actions are carried out only when predefined conditions are met. AI enhances these contracts by incorporating machine learning to adapt conditions based on evolving scenarios. This flexibility ensures operations remain secure and efficient, even in dynamic markets.

Furthermore, data integrity is critical for any financial system. Blockchain ensures data stored is tamper-proof and consistent across the network. AI complements this by analyzing data integrity and ensuring that inputs into the blockchain are accurate. It provides predictive insights and detects potential data breaches before they become critical, thus preserving the sanctity of the financial information processed.

The role of AI in enhancing cybersecurity is particularly crucial. As cyber threats grow in sophistication, static defense measures are no longer sufficient. AI-driven systems have the capacity to learn from each interaction, adapting and improving threat detection and response times continuously. Blockchain adds an additional layer by ensuring data transmitted within the network remains secure and unaltered.

Yet, integrating AI and blockchain isn't without its challenges. The computational power required to process AI operations on blockchain networks can be significant. Efficient data sharing and processing solutions need development to ensure sustainability. However, innovations in distributed computing and quantum technologies promise to alleviate some of these constraints, paving the way for more seamless integrations.

On an institutional level, the adoption of blockchain and AI can redefine risk management practices. Through predictive analytics, AI can assess market trends and predict volatilities, while blockchain records transactional histories, offering an accurate reflection of risks in real-time. This proximity to data enables a more nuanced approach to risk, allowing financial entities to make decisions that are not only informed but also strategically aligned.

The potential for improved compliance is another area where blockchain and AI shine. Regulatory environments demand meticulous reporting and adherence to guidelines, which can be cumbersome and prone to human error. Blockchain-based ledgers provide an easily auditable trail, while AI systems ensure compliance through continuous monitoring and alerting systems. This synergy reduces the administrative burden and enhances the accuracy of compliance measures.

In summary, the amalgamation of blockchain technology and artificial intelligence heralds a new paradigm in financial efficiency and security. Their combined capabilities offer not just incremental improvements, but transformative change—ushering in systems that are faster, more secure, and incredibly resilient. As technological advancements continue to bridge existing gaps, the promise of a more secure and efficient financial ecosystem stands not only as an aspiration but as a foreseeable reality.

As we explore this groundbreaking intersection, it's clear that the future of finance will be defined by innovation that transcends traditional practices, creating an infrastructure tailored for the complexities of modern economies. This integration encourages a financial future that's not just technologically advanced but inherently secure and efficient. The promise held by the fusion of blockchain and AI in finance is not merely theoretical—it is a burgeoning reality, one that holds the keys to a robust, secure, and equitable marketplace.

Chapter 9:
Fraud Detection and Prevention

In an era where financial transactions increasingly occur in digital realms, fraud detection and prevention have become crucial components of securing the financial industry. With the aid of artificial intelligence, traditional methods of spotting fraudulent activities have evolved dramatically. AI techniques now offer financial institutions the ability to analyze vast datasets swiftly, identifying anomalies and patterns that humans might miss. This technological advancement not only enhances accuracy in fraud detection but also allows real-time monitoring and response, reducing potential losses. Machine learning algorithms learn and adapt to new fraud tactics, effectively closing gaps that criminals might exploit. The role of AI in this context extends beyond mere identification; it empowers prevention strategies to be proactive rather than reactive, thus fortifying the integrity of financial operations against the ever-present threat of fraud. By integrating AI into their security protocols, financial entities can safeguard customer trust while maintaining robust defenses against illicit activities.

AI Techniques for Detecting Fraud

In the realm of financial services, fraud has been a persistent challenge that costs billions annually and erodes trust between service providers and consumers. With the rise of digital transactions and sophisticated cybercriminal tactics, traditional methods of detecting fraud are often inadequate. Fortunately, artificial intelligence offers innovative solutions that can enhance the detection and prevention of fraudulent activities, creating a safer financial environment.

AI techniques have revolutionized how financial institutions approach fraud detection. Machine learning models, in particular, are at the forefront, enabling the processing of vast amounts of transaction data to identify patterns and anomalies that might indicate fraudulent activities. These models can learn from past fraud instances, improving their accuracy over time. Unlike rule-based systems that require manual updates to detect new fraud tactics, machine learning models adapt autonomously to evolving risks.

Supervised learning is one prominent AI technique used in fraud detection. It involves training a model on a labeled dataset where instances of fraud and legitimate transactions are clearly marked. By learning the features associated with each class, the model can then classify unseen transactions in real-time. However, this method depends heavily on the availability of comprehensive and accurate historical data, which isn't always available.

Unsupervised learning offers an alternative when labeling data is challenging. Techniques like clustering and anomaly detection come into play, grouping transactions into clusters to identify outliers that don't conform to standard patterns. These outliers could signify potential fraud. The advantage here is the ability to detect novel fraud strategies without needing labeled data. However, distinguishing between truly fraudulent activities and legitimate deviations remains a significant challenge.

Another approach, deep learning, particularly excels in fraud detection due to its ability to handle complex relationships in data. For instance, neural networks can process multiple features of a transaction in parallel, identifying intricate patterns that simpler models might miss. Recurrent neural networks (RNNs) and long short-term memory (LSTM) networks are particularly effective, as they consider the sequence of transactions, helping to identify fraudulent activities occurring over time.

Beyond these core machine learning techniques, natural language processing (NLP) is used to analyze textual data linked to transactions, such as descriptions and notes. Fraudsters often manipulate transaction descriptions to mask illicit activity. NLP models help by flagging suspicious language patterns, further enhancing detection capabilities.

AI techniques also allow for real-time fraud detection, a critical aspect given the speed at which digital transactions occur. Unlike traditional methods that may result in delays, AI-powered systems analyze transactions as they happen, enabling immediate responses to prevent fraudulent activities from completing. This real-time capability is vital in high-velocity fields like e-commerce and online banking.

Despite these advances, the deployment of AI in fraud detection is not without its challenges. One significant concern is the risk of false positives, where legitimate transactions are incorrectly flagged as fraudulent. Such errors can inconvenience customers and damage the credibility of the financial institution. Thus, striking a balance between sensitivity and specificity is crucial, and AI systems must be continuously refined to minimize these incidences.

To address the shortcomings of individual models, ensemble techniques are often employed. These techniques combine multiple models to improve predictive performance. By leveraging the strengths of different models, ensemble methods such as boosting and bagging can achieve higher accuracy and reduce the likelihood of false positives and negatives.

Financial institutions are increasingly using AI to perform cross-validation checks, a technique that splits the dataset into distinct training and testing sets multiple times. This helps ensure that the fraud detection model maintains robust performance across varying datasets, making it more reliable in real-world applications.

Ethical AI is another vital consideration. Bias in AI systems can lead to discriminatory outcomes, particularly if the historical data used to train models reflect existing societal biases. Institutions need to employ fairness-aware machine learning techniques, ensuring that fraud detection systems make decisions transparently and without prejudice.

Moreover, AI systems should be designed to provide explanations for their decisions, especially in fraud detection where the stakes are high. Explainable AI (XAI) techniques aim to make the decision-making process of AI models understandable to human operators. This not only increases trust but also enables operators to verify and investigate flagged transactions more effectively.

The constant evolution of cyber threats means that AI fraud detection systems must be dynamic, continually learning from new threats and adapting to new fraud patterns. This requires not just advanced algorithms but also a forward-looking strategy encompassing continuous monitoring, updating, and validating the AI models deployed.

Collaboration between tech developers, financial practitioners, and regulatory bodies is essential to scaling AI-driven fraud solutions effectively. It ensures that the systems respect consumer privacy and comply with regulations like GDPR and the CCPA, which dictate how personal data can be used and stored.

As we look to the future, AI's role in fraud detection will likely expand further, integrating more seamlessly with blockchain technologies and the Internet of Things (IoT). These integrations might offer additional layers of security, enhancing authenticity checks and pinpointing fraudulent activity across decentralized networks.

The convergence of AI with other advanced technologies will demand a new wave of innovation in fraud prevention strategies, paving the way for a future where digital financial systems not only promise convenience and efficiency but also robust security against fraud. Financial institutions that embrace these technologies stand to benefit immensely, not only by reducing fraud but also by enhancing consumer trust in an increasingly digital economy.

Improving Fraud Detection Accuracy

In the world of finance, the term 'fraud' sends shivers up the spines of institutions and investors alike. It's a menace that's been persistently evolving alongside financial technologies. As fraud attempts become more sophisticated, the arsenal of tools and techniques aimed at combating them must also advance. Artificial intelligence has emerged as a formidable ally in this ongoing battle, shining a spotlight on the importance of improving fraud detection accuracy.

The dynamic nature of fraud schemes requires adaptive and responsive solutions. Algorithms that were effective yesterday might not detect new patterns of deceit today. This calls for systems that are not only robust but also capable of learning and evolving independently. Machine learning, a subset of AI, provides this capability by allowing systems to learn from data, identify patterns, and make decisions with minimal human intervention.

One significant advantage of AI in fraud detection is its ability to process vast amounts of data at unprecedented speeds. Consider the sheer volume of transactions processed daily by financial institutions. Humans can't feasibly monitor each transaction for signs of fraud. AI systems, however, can scour through millions of transactions instantly, flagging abnormalities that might elude a human eye.

The process begins with the integration of AI systems into existing financial infrastructures. These systems undergo a training phase, where they're exposed to historical transaction data. During this phase, the algorithms learn to distinguish between legitimate and fraudulent transactions. As they process more data, their detection capabilities become sharper and more nuanced, allowing for a proactive approach to identifying potential fraud.

It's essential to acknowledge that data is the backbone of these machine learning models. While algorithms can be inherently powerful, their efficacy is tied directly to the quality of data they're trained on. Financial institutions must ensure that their data sets are as comprehensive and representative as possible, incorporating diverse transaction types and fraud scenarios.

AI's flexibility also permits continuous updates and enhancements. This means that when new types of fraud are identified, these systems can be retrained to recognize and counteract these threats. This adaptability ensures that AI-driven tools remain ahead of fraudsters, providing a dynamic line of defense in a constantly shifting landscape.

Fraud detection isn't without its challenges, however. Over-reliance on AI can lead to a dangerous level of complacency. AI isn't infallible; false positives and negatives remain critical issues. A mismatch, where legitimate transactions are flagged as fraudulent or vice versa, can lead to both customer dissatisfaction and financial loss. Hence, it's crucial for institutions to strike a balance between automated and manual fraud screening processes.

Another layer to consider is the ethical use of AI in fraud detection. As these systems analyze data, they must adhere to strict privacy regulations, ensuring sensitive customer information remains protected. Financial institutions are thus tasked with implementing stringent data governance frameworks alongside their AI solutions. This ensures that while fraud detection capabilities grow, customer trust and privacy are never compromised.

AI's role in improving fraud detection accuracy isn't confined to real-time transaction monitoring. Financial institutions are also leveraging AI for predictive analysis. By examining historical data, AI models can forecast potential future fraud trends, enabling businesses to reinforce their defenses proactively. This forward-looking approach shifts the paradigm from reactive measures to anticipatory strategies.

Moreover, collaboration plays a crucial role in enhancing fraud detection capabilities. Financial institutions, technology providers, and regulatory bodies must work together to develop standardized frameworks for AI applications in fraud detection. By sharing insights and data, these stakeholders can collectively build stronger systems that are universally effective.

The pursuit of improving fraud detection accuracy through AI is not merely a technological endeavor; it's a strategic imperative. In a world where the financial landscape continues to evolve rapidly, institutions can't afford to lag in their defenses. AI provides the tools necessary to stay one step ahead of sophisticated fraud schemes, but it's imperative to maintain a holistic approach that combines technology, ethics, and collaboration.

As the financial industry continues to embrace AI, the potential for innovation and improvement in fraud detection knows no bounds. With continuous advancements in technology, finance professionals, tech enthusiasts, and investors find themselves at the forefront of a transformative era, poised to reap the benefits of enhanced security and accuracy in fraud detection.

Chapter 10:
Ethical Considerations
in Financial AI

As AI technologies become deeply embedded in the financial ecosystem, the question of ethics looms ever larger, demanding careful navigation to ensure these tools operate fairly and transparently. Ethical challenges arise because AI systems, despite their potential for enhanced efficiency and accuracy, can inadvertently perpetuate biases present in historical data or the algorithms themselves. This dilemma necessitates a proactive approach towards developing guidelines to build trustworthy AI systems that foster consumer confidence rather than erode it. Financial professionals must grapple with complex issues like privacy, data security, and the potential for discriminatory practices—problems that have no easy solutions, but require a concerted effort from both technology developers and financial institutions. Ignoring these ethical facets could lead to not only reputational damage but also significant regulatory repercussions. Therefore, a balanced approach that marries innovation with responsibility becomes pivotal, as we strive to harness AI's strengths while diligently mitigating its ethical risks in the financial sector.

Navigating Ethical Challenges

As AI continues to reshape the financial landscape, it brings with it a suite of ethical challenges that finance professionals can't afford to overlook. Navigating these challenges isn't just about compliance; it's about making thoughtful decisions that have real-world impacts on people and the economy. AI systems in finance are powerful tools designed to optimize investments, assess credit risk, detect fraud, and provide personalized financial advice. However, their capabilities raise serious questions about privacy, accountability, and fairness.

One of the primary ethical concerns is the potential for bias in AI algorithms. Financial AI systems often learn from large datasets that reflect existing societal biases, which can inadvertently perpetuate discrimination in credit scoring, loan approvals, and other critical financial decisions. For instance, biased training data can lead to marginalized groups being systematically disadvantaged, even if the AI systems weren't intentionally programmed to discriminate. Addressing these biases requires a multi-faceted approach that includes refining data collection methods, implementing transparency in AI decisions, and continuously auditing AI systems for fairness.

The issue of privacy is also a significant concern. Financial AI systems process vast amounts of personal data to offer accurate predictions and personalized services. This data aggregation poses a risk to consumer privacy, as unauthorized access or misuse of sensitive financial data can lead to severe consequences such as identity theft or fraud. To navigate this challenge, financial institutions must establish robust data protection protocols and ensure transparency in how consumer data is managed. Incorporating privacy-by-design principles in AI systems development can also help in safeguarding user information.

Accountability is another critical aspect of ethical AI in finance. When AI systems make automated decisions that affect people's financial lives, determining responsibility becomes complex. If an AI-driven financial decision leads to an error or harm, who should be held accountable—the developer who created the algorithm, the financial institution that deployed it, or the AI system itself? Clear accountability frameworks are necessary to address these dilemmas and ensure that financial institutions take responsibility for AI-driven outcomes. This might involve setting up oversight mechanisms and ethical review boards to evaluate AI decision-making processes.

Transparency is closely tied to accountability and is essential for building trust in financial AI systems. For finance professionals and consumers alike, understanding how an AI system arrives at a decision is crucial. However, the complexity of some AI models, especially deep learning algorithms, can make them appear as black boxes, with decision-making processes that are opaque even to the developers. Ensuring transparency may require developing explainable AI systems that can provide insights into their decision-making mechanics without compromising proprietary information.

Another ethical challenge in financial AI is the risk of over-reliance. With AI becoming deeply embedded in financial operations, there's a danger of diminishing human oversight. Over-reliance on AI systems can lead to complacency, where professionals might accept AI outputs without critical evaluation. This can be problematic if AI systems make decisions based on flawed data or algorithms. Balancing AI automation with human judgment is essential to mitigate risks and ensure that AI systems complement, rather than replace, human expertise.

The rapid pace of AI advancement also poses ethical challenges related to job displacement. As AI automates routine tasks in the finance sector, concerns about workforce reduction and job losses emerge. However, it's also an opportunity for upskilling and reskilling the workforce, encouraging finance professionals to develop new skills that complement AI technologies. Financial institutions must proactively manage this transition to minimize negative social impacts and promote a future where humans and AI systems work harmoniously.

Navigating these ethical challenges requires a proactive and collaborative approach between regulators, financial institutions, technologists, and consumers. Regulatory bodies play a crucial role in establishing frameworks that promote ethical AI use. They must keep pace with AI innovations and develop guidelines that protect consumer interests while fostering innovation. Collaborative efforts between industry stakeholders can lead to the development of best practices and standards that ensure AI technologies are ethically sound and beneficial to society.

In conclusion, the ethical challenges posed by AI in finance are multifaceted and require continuous attention and adaptation. As AI systems evolve, so too must the strategies and frameworks for addressing ethical dilemmas. Financial institutions, regulators, and other stakeholders must remain vigilant, anticipating potential ethical issues and implementing robust measures to mitigate risks. By doing so, they can harness the power of AI to drive innovation, efficiency, and inclusion in the financial sector while upholding the highest ethical standards.

Building Trustworthy AI Systems

As artificial intelligence continues to weave itself into the fabric of the financial industry, the notion of trust takes on newfound significance. But what does it mean to build trustworthy AI systems in finance? At its core, trust in AI systems is anchored in transparency, accountability, and reliability. These principles serve as critical guideposts in ensuring that AI-driven solutions do not merely perform their intended tasks but do so under the rigors of ethical responsibility and fairness.

The journey toward trustworthy AI begins with transparency. In financial applications, transparency isn't just a desirable feature—it's a necessity. A lack of clarity in how AI systems make decisions can foster mistrust and skepticism among stakeholders. For example, when algorithms dictate creditworthiness or investment decisions, stakeholders need to know the "why" behind these choices. Providing clear explanations of decision-making processes can mitigate confusion and suspicion, opening the door to broader acceptance and trust.

Transparency, however, is not easily achieved. The complexity of AI models, particularly deep learning architectures, can make interpretation challenging. Despite these hurdles, organizations can adopt practices such as model documentation and interpretability techniques—tools designed to shed light on black-box models. By offering insights into how input data influences outcomes, these tools help demystify AI processes, aligning them more closely with human understanding.

Accountability forms the second pillar of trustworthy AI systems. In the financial industry, decision-making often involves significant economic implications. Whether an algorithm is assessing risk, recommending trades, or managing client portfolios, accountability ensures that there is always a human overseeing AI's actions. This stewardship is crucial in defining who bears responsibility when AI systems falter, as accountability cannot be relegated to a machine. Financial institutions must clearly delineate roles and establish governance frameworks that ensure human oversight complements AI efficacy.

With accountability anchored, the conversation inevitably turns to reliability. In finance, the stakes are incredibly high, with reputations and fortunes often riding on AI's performance. A reliable AI system consistently delivers accurate and unbiased outcomes that stakeholders can count on. This reliability underpins trust, fostering confidence in the system's ability to perform under varied conditions without significant deviation from expected behavior.

However, the pursuit of reliability is fraught with challenges. AI systems are prone to biases, stemming from skewed training data, flawed algorithms, or systemic biases embedded in financial markets. Addressing these biases entails a multifaceted approach involving rigorous testing, diverse data collection, and regular audits. Such measures can spotlight anomalies and enable corrective actions, strengthening the foundation of trustworthiness over time.

Continually evaluating AI systems against fairness benchmarks is another crucial step in building trustworthy solutions. Fairness in AI isn't simply about evenhandedness in outcomes but ensuring fairness in opportunity and treatment. As systems often make pivotal decisions affecting people's lives, like credit approvals or investment advice, it's essential that they do so equitably. Financial institutions must regularly assess algorithms for any unintended negative impacts on specific groups, making necessary adjustments to rectify disparities.

Gaining the trust of users also involves grappling with AI's inherent limitations. Beyond acknowledging AI's potential, it's paramount to convey its boundaries—contexts where AI decisions may lack nuance compared to human judgment, or situations warranting human intervention. By realistically setting expectations, financial institutions can avoid overpromising, thereby building a more authentic trust based on informed understanding rather than blind faith.

Security is another cornerstone of trust in AI systems. With vast amounts of sensitive data at play, safeguarding this information from breaches becomes a top priority. Robust digital security protocols need to be intertwined with AI architectures to prevent unauthorized access or data leaks. Encrypted communications, secure data storage, and real-time threat detection mechanisms work in tandem to uphold data integrity—a crucial ingredient for trust.

Moreover, establishing trust in AI requires a collaborative effort across the organization. Engaging stakeholders, including clients, regulators, and internal teams, in dialogue about AI strategies fosters transparency and builds confidence. Open communication channels allow stakeholders to express concerns and insights, promoting a co-creation approach in refining and evolving AI applications.

Regulators also play a pivotal role in the establishment of trustworthy AI finance systems. By devising clear guidelines and regulations surrounding AI deployments, they offer a framework within which financial entities must operate, ensuring uniformity and fairness. Compliance with these regulations assures stakeholders that AI systems aren't developed in isolation but adhere to collective societal norms and standards.

In conclusion, constructing trustworthy AI systems in the financial sector is a formidable task, requiring continuous commitment and iterative improvements. Through transparency, accountability, and reliability, alongside a focus on fairness and security, financial institutions can foster trust not just in their AI applications but in the broader promise of AI itself. As the sector progresses, these guiding principles will play a pivotal role in ensuring that AI not only enhances financial services but does so in a socially responsible and ethical manner.

Chapter 11:
The Regulatory Landscape

The intersection of artificial intelligence and finance is not just a technological revolution but also a regulatory challenge, as governing bodies around the world grapple with the complexities posed by this burgeoning field. Existing regulations, often designed for traditional financial systems, are being stretched to address the novel risks and opportunities that AI presents. As AI systems increasingly make autonomous decisions that affect economic markets, regulatory frameworks must evolve to ensure transparency, accountability, and ethical use. Financial institutions face the dual challenge of integrating AI technologies while navigating a maze of compliance standards that vary across jurisdictions. Future regulatory landscapes are likely to introduce stricter protocols and innovative guidelines, particularly focused on data privacy, decision-making biases, and system security. For finance professionals, staying ahead in the AI game isn't just about adopting new technologies but also about understanding and preparing for the regulatory shifts that will inevitably shape the industry's future. Such preparation ensures that AI's integration into finance doesn't just drive growth but does so in a manner that is responsible and sustainable, protecting stakeholders and maintaining trust in financial markets.

Current Regulations Affecting AI in Finance

The intersection of artificial intelligence (AI) and finance isn't just about innovation and progress; it's also about navigating a complex regulatory landscape. As AI increasingly permeates financial services, governments and institutions worldwide are striving to develop regulations that ensure fairness, transparency, and security. These regulations are vital in balancing the potential of AI with safeguarding public interests.

AI can significantly enhance financial services, but it's accompanied by risks such as bias, data privacy issues, and a lack of transparency, commonly seen in "black-box" algorithms. Consequently, regulators have a challenging task. They need to protect consumers and ensure market stability while encouraging innovation. The regulatory environment is continually evolving, aiming to address the implications of AI-driven decision-making in the financial sector.

The United States and the European Union lead the regulatory efforts in this space. In the US, the Securities and Exchange Commission (SEC) and the Commodity Futures Trading Commission (CFTC) are at the forefront of managing AI's growing influence in finance. Their focus is on safeguarding investor interests and market integrity. Meanwhile, in the EU, the General Data Protection Regulation (GDPR) plays a crucial role in how financial institutions handle data, impacting AI deployments that rely heavily on personal data.

Specific guidelines and frameworks are still materializing, but there's significant attention towards transparency, accountability, and fairness in AI applications. For instance, the European Commission's proposed Artificial Intelligence Act outlines strict obligations for high-risk AI systems, heavily influencing financial applications. These obligations include robust data governance, transparency, and human oversight, aiming to mitigate potential risks while fostering trust in AI systems.

Regulators are particularly vigilant about algorithmic trading, an area where AI's potential for rapid, autonomous decision-making could disrupt markets. In response, the EU's Markets in Financial Instruments Directive II (MiFID II) and the US's Dodd-Frank Act emphasize transparency in trading algorithms. These regulations require firms to disclose their trading strategies and maintain rigorous controls. This regulatory oversight is designed to prevent market abuse and ensure financial stability.

Another critical aspect is the management of AI-related risks, particularly those related to data privacy and security. The financial sector's reliance on vast amounts of data makes it a prime target for cyber threats. Consequently, regulations surrounding data protection, such as GDPR in the EU and various state laws in the US, are essential in dictating how financial institutions develop and implement AI technologies.

Implementing AI responsibly also involves addressing potential biases embedded in algorithms. Discriminatory practices, whether intentional or unintentional, pose significant ethical and legal challenges. Regulators are pushing for robust frameworks that ensure fair treatment of consumers and fair lending practices. The US Equal Credit Opportunity Act and the UK Equality Act are examples of legal structures that impact how AI is used in decision-making processes, particularly in credit scoring and lending.

As these regulations evolve, financial institutions must stay agile, ensuring compliance without stifling innovation. Many firms are adopting rigorous AI governance frameworks to navigate this. These frameworks emphasize transparency, explainability, and ethical AI use. By embedding these principles into their operations, firms aim to meet regulatory requirements while maintaining competitive advantage.

Cross-border transactions add another layer of complexity. As AI crosses geographical boundaries, inconsistencies between national regulations can create compliance challenges. Global coordination among regulators is crucial to address these challenges, ensuring seamless operations and fostering international cooperation in financial markets.

Educational initiatives play a significant role in ensuring regulatory compliance. Regulators are increasingly focusing on financial literacy surrounding AI applications. By raising awareness about AI's implications, they aim to prepare both institutions and consumers for the technological shift. Such initiatives help in aligning business practices with regulatory expectations, promoting a more informed and resilient financial ecosystem.

Future discussions will likely revolve around ethics and trust in AI. As stakeholders engage in dialogue, they aim to foster frameworks that not only comply with regulations but also address broader societal impacts. This requires collaboration between regulators, technologists, and financial institutions to create a coherent approach that enhances financial innovation while ensuring stability and security.

The path forward requires balancing the dual demands of innovation and regulation. Regulators are tasked with crafting nuanced responses that reflect AI's transformative potential and its accompanying risks. By doing so, they aim to empower financial institutions to innovate responsibly, recognizing AI's ability to reshape financial services significantly. As the regulatory landscape continues to mature, it's evident that AI's future in finance will depend heavily on the frameworks put in place today.

Future Regulatory Challenges

As artificial intelligence continues to weave itself into the intricate fabric of the financial industry, regulators grapple with the challenge of ensuring that the new landscape remains fair, transparent, and secure. The rapid pace of AI development often outstrips the ability of existing frameworks to keep up, creating a void that demands innovative approaches to regulation. Finance professionals, investors, and tech enthusiasts alike find themselves on the cusp of a transformative era where traditional boundaries are blurred, prompting an urgent need to rethink regulatory paradigms.

One of the most pressing challenges lies in the sheer scalability and opacity of AI systems. Unlike human traders or advisors, AI models can process vast swaths of data and execute decisions at speeds and volumes unimaginable to the human brain. This capability, while advantageous, poses significant risks if not properly understood and supervised. Regulators face the daunting task of crafting rules that can effectively monitor and mitigate risks without stifling innovation. The fine line between fostering technological advancement and safeguarding financial stability is thinner than ever.

Moreover, the cross-border nature of financial transactions complicates regulatory efforts. AI systems don't recognize geographical boundaries; they operate in an interconnected global market. This raises questions about jurisdiction and the alignment of international regulatory standards. How can regulators ensure compliance across different legal systems, especially when AI technologies may be developed in one country, deployed in another, and affect markets globally? It's a puzzle that demands collaborative solutions and robust dialogue between international regulatory bodies.

Data privacy and security constitute another significant challenge. Finance has always been data-driven, but the integration of AI elevates the stakes considerably. The vast datasets required to train AI models often contain sensitive financial and personal information, making them prime targets for cyberattacks. Ensuring that these systems adhere to stringent data protection standards while maintaining their efficacy is paramount. Regulators must enforce rigorous data governance policies to protect consumer information and preserve trust in financial institutions.

The issue of algorithmic transparency can't be overlooked either. AI's black-box nature — its tendency to provide results without a clear explanation process — presents a dilemma for both developers and regulators. How can regulators effectively scrutinize and understand decision-making processes that even the most astute programmers may struggle to decode? Developing frameworks that demand explainability without compromising the efficacy of the AI models is crucial. Regulators will need to define what constitutes sufficient transparency and how it can be measured and enforced.

In addition to transparency, there's the challenge of accountability. Determining liability when an AI system makes an error or produces biased results is a complex conundrum. Traditional financial regulations were designed with human actors in mind, leaving gaps when applied to AI-driven processes. Who is to blame when an algorithm trades poorly, perhaps triggered by unforeseen market conditions or embedded biases? Should liability rest with the developers, the financial institutions employing the AI, or perhaps the regulators who failed to envisage such scenarios?

Bias and fairness are areas ripe for regulatory oversight. Despite advances in AI, biases in data and algorithms persist, sometimes reinforcing systemic inequalities. In the financial sector, this could manifest as biased lending practices or unfair trading advantages. Regulators need to establish clear guidelines on identifying and mitigating bias within AI systems, ensuring compliance and fairness across all financial products and services. Developing such regulations is not straightforward; it requires understanding the nuances of machine learning and the sources of bias within data used for training.

As AI creates innovative financial products, new types of risk emerge. The history of finance is replete with examples of products that were poorly understood and inadequately regulated until after they caused significant disruption. Regulators must proactively anticipate the next generation of financial innovations and their implications, adopting forward-thinking approaches rather than reactive measures. This anticipatory regulation demands a deep understanding of technology and an ability to foresee potential disruptions.

Regulatory technology, or "RegTech," could serve as a tool to address these challenges. By leveraging AI to enhance regulatory compliance and monitoring, regulators can gain more granular insights into financial activity in real time. This could lead to a paradigm shift, where regulation is not just about enforcement but also empowers institutions to understand and manage risks more effectively. RegTech could therefore bridge the gap between rapid innovation and regulatory oversight, though its adoption will require regulators to be adept with AI themselves.

In addressing these regulatory challenges, collaboration between various stakeholders is critical. Financial institutions, tech companies, regulators, and academic researchers must share insights and collaborate on best practices to create sustainable regulatory frameworks. Such cooperation could lead to the development of standards and protocols that ensure AI serves the broader goals of equity, stability, and efficiency in the financial markets.

In conclusion, the future of financial regulation in an AI-driven world is one of constant vigilance and adaptability. As AI continues to evolve, so too must the regulatory frameworks that ensure its safe and equitable deployment. Finance professionals, tech enthusiasts, and policymakers must work together to navigate these uncharted waters, transforming regulatory challenges into opportunities for innovation and improvement. The task is daunting, yet critical, for shaping a financial future that balances technological advancement with the principles of fairness and accountability.

Chapter 12:
AI in Personal Finance

As AI steadily permeates the sphere of personal finance, it's transforming how individuals manage their money, reshaping tasks that once required manual effort and constant vigilance. With sophisticated algorithms and machine learning techniques, personal financial management becomes streamlined, offering users the ability to automate budgeting, track expenses, and optimize saving strategies with precision. Intelligent tools can analyze spending habits, suggest allocation adjustments, and even predict financial trends, all tailored to an individual's lifestyle. As these technologies mature, they empower users to make informed decisions and maintain financial health effortlessly, fostering a future where financial independence is attainable through the seamless integration of AI in daily life.

Automating Personal Financial Management

In the sprawling landscape of personal finance, the integration of artificial intelligence is revolutionizing how individuals manage their money. Automated financial systems are no longer the exclusive domain of large investment firms or high-net-worth individuals. Now, they're increasingly commonplace among everyday consumers looking to streamline their financial responsibilities.

AI-based tools simplify tasks ranging from bill payment to sophisticated investment management, transforming the way people interact with their finances.

Traditionally, managing finances required a significant amount of time and expertise. Keeping track of expenses, optimally allocating savings, or rebalancing a portfolio meant laborious calculations and deep analysis. Many sought the counsel of financial advisors or relied on personal spreadsheets, but both options came with limitations. Financial advisors could be expensive and sometimes out of reach for the average consumer, while manual tracking through spreadsheets often left room for human error and cumbersome data entry.

This is where AI-based solutions come into play, providing custom-tailored financial advice at a fraction of the cost. With their ability to process vast amounts of data quickly and accurately, AI systems help in creating efficient budgeting plans. They adjust spending habits by categorizing transactions in real-time, offering insights that human analysis might miss. Such automatic categorizations allow users to see at a glance where their money goes, leading to more informed financial decisions.

Automation doesn't stop with budgeting. AI also plays a crucial role in managing debt. Many platforms use AI algorithms to recommend optimal debt repayment strategies. By analyzing various debts' interest rates and monthly income streams, these systems can prioritize which loans to pay off first, often saving users thousands of dollars in interest payments over time. In managing credit, AI tools detect patterns and offer suggestions for improving credit scores, providing actionable recommendations and monitoring credit report changes to alert users of any potential fraud.

Moreover, the scope of AI in personal financial management extends into investment management. Robo-advisors have democratized access to investment opportunities, once reserved for the well-connected. These platforms use AI to construct and manage portfolios based on individual risk tolerance and financial goals, balancing risk and return in a way that aligns with each user's preferences. They keep emotional biases out of the decision-making process, which can substantially boost long-term returns. As market conditions change, robo-advisors automatically rebalance portfolios to maintain optimal asset allocation, reducing the manual intervention required.

AI's predictive capabilities are another boon for personal finance automation. Predictive analytics look at historical data and current spending patterns to forecast future financial needs. With this information, automated systems can send timely alerts about when funds might be low or when upcoming expenses are due, helping users avoid overdraft fees and ensure sufficient liquidity.
Such forecasts make it easier to set up automatic savings plans where a specific portion of income is transferred into savings or investment accounts, nudging people to save more effectively.

The element of personal finance most susceptible to oversight is arguably bill payment. Forgetting to pay a bill or underpaying can result in penalties or adversely affect one's credit score. AI-driven reminder systems, integrated with calendar apps, proactively manage due dates and amounts owed, sending notifications to ensure timely payments. In some cases, these systems can directly execute payments, further eliminating the risk of human error or negligence.

With security always a top concern, AI enhances data protection through fraud detection algorithms. These algorithms continuously monitor transactions for suspicious activity, looking for anomalies that deviate from established patterns. Integrated into personal banking apps, they ensure rapid response to unauthorized transactions, giving users peace of mind.
Complex algorithms within these systems filter noise from real threats, ensuring alerts are timely and relevant.

The personalization capability in AI systems is continually improving, offering users a more customized experience of managing their financial life. Through natural language processing, interfaces understand and respond to user queries in a conversational manner, making financial management less intimidating for those less tech-savvy.

As AI systems learn from past interactions, their advice becomes increasingly pertinent, offering suggestions more aligned with users' evolving financial landscapes.

However, it's important to recognize challenges alongside advancements. The reliance on automated systems relinquishes some control from users, potentially leading to over-dependence on technology. There's also the inherent necessity for data privacy, as integrating all financial accounts into one platform presents exposure risks. Securing these systems against breaches remains a critical priority, as they hold sensitive user data.

Furthermore, the 'one-size-fits-all' nature of some solutions may overlook unique financial situations, requiring human oversight to ensure absolute suitability.

In the realm of personal finance, AI promises both precision and convenience, unveiling a future where managing money is not just less complex, but also more effective. The traditional 'set it and forget it' mindset transforms into a dynamic ongoing process guided by the latest data-driven insights. As AI technology continues to evolve, the inefficiencies in personal financial management are gradually being ironed out, leading to smarter financial habits and improved financial health for individuals worldwide. The future, as it unveils itself, seems brighter when AI holds the fiscal helm, steering it with an accuracy honed to individual needs and goals.

AI Tools for Budgeting and Saving

Artificial intelligence isn't just shaking up investment strategies and risk management; it's also making significant inroads into personal finance, particularly in budgeting and saving. With the advent of AI-driven tools and applications, individuals now have unparalleled assistance in managing their finances, creating budgets, and optimizing savings. These technologies don't just make personal finance management more accessible; they transform it into a more strategic and proactive process.

AI tools in budgeting leverage machine learning and data analytics to offer tailored financial advice. By analyzing spending patterns and historical financial data, these tools can forecast future expenses, identify unnecessary expenditures, and suggest potential savings. Unlike traditional budgeting methods that often require extensive manual tracking, AI-driven solutions offer an automated approach. This level of automation helps take the guesswork out of financial planning, providing users with clear and actionable insights into their spending habits.

One remarkable development in this sphere is the personalization of financial advice. Historically, financial advice was a one-size-fits-all affair, rarely customized to suit unique individual needs. Today, AI enables highly individualized guidance. AI algorithms can assess a user's financial status and preferences, offering bespoke suggestions that fit diverse financial situations and goals. This personalized advice can range from changing spending habits to optimizing investment portfolios, proving invaluable for those looking to make informed financial decisions without the need for a personal financial advisor.

Moreover, AI tools often integrate seamlessly with existing financial ecosystems. Many banks and financial institutions now offer AI-powered applications that connect directly with users' bank accounts and credit cards, providing a real-time overview of all financial activities. These integrations allow for immediate alerts on overspending, real-time improvement suggestions, and even reminders for upcoming bills. This immediacy ensures users are always aware of their financial standing, enabling proactive adjustments to their financial behavior when necessary.

Saving money is another area where AI tools excel. Automated savings apps, powered by AI, can analyze an individual's financial behavior to determine optimal times and amounts for saving. These applications utilize algorithms to automatically move small, non-disruptive amounts from checking to savings accounts, based on the user's spending habits and cash flow patterns. Over time, these small amounts accumulate, building significant savings with minimal impact on day-to-day financial activities.

In addition to individualized savings plans, many AI tools offer educational components, empowering users to better understand their financial landscapes. In-app tutorials, personalized financial tips, and access to resource libraries on financial literacy are becoming standard features. By educating users, these tools not only enhance the in-the-moment financial decisions but also improve long-term financial skills. This dual approach of active management and education creates a comprehensive financial empowerment package.

This transformation in personal finance is greatly enhanced by voice-activated AI platforms. Innovators have integrated voice recognition capabilities into financial management tools, allowing users to interact with their financial data as naturally as if they were conversing with a human advisor. With simple voice commands, users can check account balances, review recent transactions, or adjust budgetary allocations conveniently without needing to navigate complicated app interfaces.

Security, naturally, is a crucial concern in incorporating these advanced technologies. AI budgeting tools are fortified with state-of-the-art encryption and security protocols to safeguard personal financial data. Robust authentication methods, often driven by AI such as biometric recognition, add an extra layer of protection. These measures ensure that while financial data is more interconnected than ever, it remains as secure as it is easily accessible to the rightful owner.

One cannot discuss AI in budgeting and saving solutions without mentioning the democratization of financial planning. With the proliferation of free and low-cost AI-based apps, more people than ever before have access to sophisticated financial management tools. These cost-effective solutions break down barriers that traditionally made financial advisory exclusive to the affluent, allowing broader audiences to benefit from the opportunities once available only through costly financial consultancy.

However, the rapid growth of AI tools in personal finance isn't without its challenges. There's an ongoing debate about data privacy and ethical use of user data. Financial institutions and tech companies must ensure transparency in how they utilize user information to fuel AI algorithms. Trust becomes a currency, as users must be aware and comfortable with the data practices of the platforms they employ. Ensuring that these concerns are addressed is paramount to the continued adoption and success of AI in personal finance.

AI-driven budgeting and saving tools represent a dynamic shift in how individuals engage with their finances. As these technologies evolve, their integration into daily financial practices will become increasingly seamless and sophisticated, offering unmatched assistance in navigating personal finances. These tools not only enhance financial literacy and decision-making but also empower individuals to achieve greater financial stability and freedom. In this light, AI's role in budgeting and saving is not just supportive; it's revolutionary.

Chapter 13:
The Role of AI in Corporate Finance

AI is fundamentally reshaping corporate finance by enhancing the precision and efficacy of strategic financial planning and operations. Businesses are increasingly leveraging AI to analyze vast datasets, revealing insights that drive more informed decision-making processes. AI's ability to forecast future trends helps corporations optimize their resource allocation, ensuring that they can navigate market volatility with agility and confidence. Moreover, in mergers and acquisitions, AI tools accelerate due diligence, offering predictive analytics and risk assessments that streamline negotiations and valuations. With AI, financial leaders gain a competitive edge, using intelligent automation to boost efficiency while reducing operational costs. This fusion of technology and finance paves the way for more resilient, agile, and strategic corporate environments. As AI continues to evolve, its integration will be indispensable in maintaining the dynamism required for thriving in today's fast-paced economic landscape.

Strategic Financial Planning with AI

In the evolving landscape of corporate finance, strategic financial planning stands as a cornerstone for sustainable growth and informed decision-making. Artificial Intelligence is redefining this aspect with unprecedented precision and adaptability. As organizations navigate complex financial terrains, AI acts not just as a tool but as a transformative ally. By harnessing AI, companies can forecast with greater accuracy, identify growth opportunities, and mitigate risks like never before.

AI offers the capability to analyze large volumes of data rapidly and extract actionable insights. Traditional methods of financial planning relied heavily on historical data and intuition. Today, AI systems integrate various data sources including real-time market trends, economic indicators, and company-specific factors, providing a 360-degree view of potential financial scenarios. This dynamic assessment allows for adaptive strategies that can accommodate volatile market conditions.

At its core, AI-driven financial planning emphasizes data-driven decision-making. Advanced algorithms process thousands of variables simultaneously, identifying patterns and correlations that may elude human analysts. This deep analysis fosters a predictive approach, helping organizations anticipate market shifts and adjust their strategies proactively. Instead of reacting to market changes, companies can position themselves to take advantage of emerging trends.

The role of AI in budgeting and forecasting is particularly noteworthy. AI algorithms can evaluate historical performance and current economic conditions to project future financial outcomes. This is achieved through techniques like neural networks and decision trees that enhance forecasting precision. Automated forecasting models provide finance professionals with tools to predict revenue, optimize cash flow, and allocate resources more efficiently, ensuring long-term financial health.

Moreover, AI introduces a level of customization that was previously unattainable. Companies can create highly tailored financial strategies that align with their specific goals and industry nuances. For instance, scenario analysis tools powered by AI allow decision-makers to simulate various financial conditions and their potential impacts.

These simulations help in crafting strategic responses, enhancing the firm's resilience to financial shocks.

Risk management, a critical component of financial planning, is significantly bolstered by AI. Machine learning models can detect and quantify risks with impressive accuracy. By evaluating diverse risk factors and their probabilistic outcomes, AI aids in constructing comprehensive risk mitigation strategies. These AI-driven insights enable finance teams to allocate capital judiciously, balancing risk and reward in a structured manner.

AI also facilitates strategic mergers and acquisitions planning, giving businesses an upper hand in identifying potential opportunities. Machine learning tools assess potential targets, aligning them with a company's strategic objectives and financial capabilities. By analyzing growth patterns, financial health, and industry position, AI supports due diligence processes, ensuring that mergers and acquisitions create value rather than unforeseen liabilities.

In strategic financial planning, the adaptability of AI means staying ahead in an increasingly competitive market. Organizations that leverage the full spectrum of AI capabilities find themselves better equipped to navigate the financial landscape. Whether through enhancing predictive accuracy, optimizing resource allocation, or fortifying risk management, AI's impact is both profound and wide-reaching.

Nevertheless, integrating AI into financial planning comes with its own challenges. It requires significant investment in technology and a shift in organizational culture. Companies must dedicate resources to training and developing AI-compatible systems while ensuring they adhere to stringent regulatory frameworks. However, the benefits of AI vastly outweigh these initial hurdles, as evidenced by the competitive edge it offers.

In conclusion, AI's role in strategic financial planning is transformative, offering unparalleled precision, adaptability, and insight. As companies continue to explore AI's potential, they unlock new avenues for strategic growth and financial stewardship. The future of corporate finance will undoubtedly be shaped by those who can adeptly weave AI into their strategic fabric, leading the charge toward innovative and sustainable financial practices.

AI in Mergers and Acquisitions

Artificial intelligence (AI) is reshaping the landscape of corporate finance, particularly in the complex arena of mergers and acquisitions (M&A). Traditionally associated with hefty spreadsheets and detailed financial analyses, M&A is evolving into a more streamlined and data-driven process thanks to AI. With AI, companies are moving beyond rote calculations to integrate predictive models, real-time data analytics, and even natural language processing (NLP) to assess potential deals swiftly and accurately. This shift not only enhances efficiency but also enables finance professionals to focus on strategic decisions rather than being bogged down by manual processes.

AI is particularly adept at handling one of the most challenging aspects of M&A: due diligence. In the past, this process involved teams of analysts sifting through mountains of documents to verify financials, assess risks, and evaluate the viability of a merger or acquisition target. Now, AI technologies such as machine learning algorithms can automate these checks by identifying patterns and anomalies in vast data sets that human eyes might miss. This ability to process and analyze vast quantities of data quickly is giving companies a competitive edge, allowing them to close deals faster than ever before.

Besides due diligence, AI is also transforming post-merger integration, which is crucial for realizing the synergies and value anticipated from a deal. AI can simulate various integration scenarios, identifying potential operational hiccups before they occur. Moreover, it can facilitate seamless communication between merged entities by suggesting ways to reconcile different legacy systems and practices. As a result, companies achieve smoother transitions, often overcoming cultural and operational challenges with greater ease.

One of the most exciting AI advancements in M&A is sentiment analysis using NLP. This tool enables acquirers to gauge the public and employee sentiment regarding the companies involved in a deal, offering insights into brand reputation and potential cultural clashes. Monitoring social media, news articles, and employee review platforms, AI can highlight contentious issues or positive perceptions that might influence the success of a merger. Such awareness can guide post-merger communication strategies, minimizing disruptions and maintaining employee morale and customer trust.

Risk assessment in M&A is becoming markedly precise with AI's infiltration into the field. Machine learning models evaluate a range of financial indicators, market conditions, and historical case studies to predict the risks associated with a merger or acquisition. These algorithms continuously learn and adapt to new data inputs, offering ever more refined insights into potential pitfalls or opportunities. For investors and decision-makers, this means a greater level of confidence when approving high-stake transactions.

Moreover, AI is enabling predictive analytics that foresee market trends and shifts, which are pivotal in shaping M&A strategies. By analyzing historical data and weighing economic indicators, AI can suggest optimal times for market entry or exit, thereby maximizing the financial benefits of a deal. This strategic foresight can be particularly beneficial amid volatile economic conditions where timing can significantly impact the success of an acquisition or merger.

Recent advancements in AI also integrate with blockchain technology to enhance transparency and security in M&A

transactions. These technologies ensure that all transaction records are immutable and verifiable, reducing the likelihood of discrepancies or fraud. As these platforms mature, they promise to foster trust among parties, making cross-border and multi-party deals more straightforward and less risky.

The implementation of AI in M&A is not without its challenges, though. Data privacy remains a pressing concern, as massive amounts of sensitive corporate data are processed during these transactions. Companies must navigate this tricky landscape, ensuring they comply with varying global data protection regulations while leveraging AI capabilities. Additionally, successful AI deployment requires a cultural shift within organizations. Teams must be willing to trust AI-driven insights and incorporate them into their decision-making processes.

As AI continues to evolve, its application in M&A is likely to broaden. In the future, AI could predict market disruptions before they happen, offering companies not just insights but strategies for navigating these changes successfully. This will require a dynamic relationship between humans and machines, where AI acts as both a guide and a partner in the complex chess game that is M&A.

In conclusion, AI's penetration into mergers and acquisitions heralds a new era of data-driven decision-making in corporate finance. While challenges remain, the potential for AI to optimize every phase of the M&A process—from initial target identification to post-merger integration—is undeniable. For finance professionals, tech enthusiasts, and investors, understanding how to harness this technology is pivotal in navigating the future financial landscape effectively.

Chapter 14:
Deep Learning and Data-
Driven Decisions

D eep learning reshapes finance by sifting through oceans of data to provide transformative insights, enabling sharper, risk-aware decision-making. This technology thrives on neural networks that mirror the human brain's capacity to learn from experience, powering applications that range from stock price forecasting to fraud detection. Financial institutions leverage these advanced models to predict trends and consumer behaviors with unprecedented accuracy, tapping into vast, diverse datasets. Deep learning's reliance on immense data quantities and model refinement underpins its effectiveness, making robust data governance and training protocols crucial. As firms embrace this technology, they gain the agility to navigate the fast-paced, data-rich financial landscape, driving strategic decisions that align with both market forces and consumer expectations.

Applications of Deep Learning in Finance

Deep learning, an advanced form of machine learning, has rapidly become a cornerstone in the landscape of finance. With its ability to unearth intricate patterns and generate insights from massive datasets, it's no wonder that financial institutions have embraced this technology to make more informed, data-driven decisions. One major application is in the realm of algorithmic trading, where deep learning models have revolutionized how trades are executed. These models can process vast quantities of data in real-time, identifying market trends and making split-second trading decisions that were previously impossible for humans to make quickly.

Besides algorithmic trading, deep learning significantly benefits portfolio management. Traditional investment strategies often involve extensive research and human intuition, but they can fall short in predicting market shifts accurately. Deep learning algorithms, however, are adept at handling mountains of historical financial data, which they use to predict stock prices, assess asset correlations, and even forecast market volatility. These algorithms refine their predictions by learning from both past and current data, improving accuracy over time as more information becomes available.

Fraud detection is another area where deep learning has made remarkable strides. Financial fraud is an ever-present risk that costs businesses and individuals billions every year. With the advent of deep learning, banks and financial institutions can now detect fraudulent activities with greater precision. By training neural networks on vast datasets of transaction history, these systems can learn to identify unusual patterns and flag transactions that deviate from the norm. This ability is especially useful in combating sophisticated fraud schemes that mutate over time, as deep learning models can adapt and recognize new manifestations of fraudulent behavior.

Moving on to risk management, deep learning plays a pivotal role in assessing and mitigating financial risks. The financial markets are inherently unstable, with numerous factors influencing their volatility. Deep learning models can digest broad datasets, from corporate earnings reports to geopolitical developments, and evaluate their potential impact on financial instruments. By combining various data sources and types, these models offer unparalleled insights into probable risks, allowing institutions to devise strategies for cushioning against adverse events.

Credit scoring and assessment have also been transformed by deep learning techniques. Traditional credit scoring models rely on a limited number of variables, such as payment history and outstanding credit, to determine an individual's creditworthiness. While this method can be effective, it often overlooks nuances present in an individual's financial behaviors. Deep learning systems, by contrast, assess a broader spectrum of data points, leading to a more comprehensive understanding of credit risk. This approach not only enhances the accuracy of credit assessments but also opens up access to credit for individuals who may have been unfairly judged by traditional models.

Furthermore, the world of financial advising is feeling the deep learning effect as well. Robo-advisors, digital platforms that provide automated financial advice, are now using deep learning to enhance their service offerings. By analyzing numerous financial inputs from the client's portfolio performance to market analytics, these platforms deliver personalized investment strategies that adapt as conditions change. This capability answers the growing demand for scalable financial advice, easing the workload on human advisors and allowing them to focus on more complex client needs.

Beyond these applications, deep learning is reshaping how financial organizations handle customer interactions. By incorporating deep learning-enabled natural language processing, customer service bots can understand and respond to inquiries more naturally, improving user experience. Additionally, these systems can identify sentiment in customer communications, pinpointing potential dissatisfaction and allowing companies to address issues preemptively.

Predictive analytics, powered by deep learning, deserves special mention as it helps finance professionals not only analyze current trends but also predict future market movements. These models synthesize data from various sources, including social media sentiment, global news, and economic indicators, to generate forecasts that inform investment decisions. As these models learn and evolve, their predictions become more refined, offering a significant competitive edge in the fast-paced world of finance.

Moreover, deep learning's potential is being explored in enhancing compliance and regulatory adherence. Financial institutions are under immense pressure to comply with ever-evolving regulations. By employing deep learning models, these organizations can automate the analysis of regulatory documents and transactions, ensuring compliance with minimal human oversight. This not only reduces the risk of non-compliance but also alleviates the regulatory burden by efficiently processing and flagging areas of concern.

In conclusion, the adoption of deep learning in finance is an exciting advance that signals a transformative shift in how financial data is analyzed and applied. The versatility of deep learning allows its application across a spectrum of functions within the financial sector, from trading and fraud detection to customer service and compliance. As these technologies continue to evolve, they are expected to further embed themselves into the core operations of financial institutions, driving a more efficient, responsive, and insightful financial landscape.

Data Sources and Model Training Techniques

In the realm of deep learning and financial decision-making, the quality of data sources and the rigor of model training techniques form the backbone of success. At the core of any deep learning model lies data—vast, diverse, and often messy. The financial industry, with its sprawling datasets, provides a fertile ground for deep learning applications. However, navigating this sea of information requires precision and strategy.

The first step in any effective deep learning venture within finance is identifying appropriate data sources. Financial data comes in various forms, such as historical stock prices, trading volumes, economic indicators, news reports, and even social media sentiment. Each type of data holds a unique key to unlocking insights if harnessed correctly. For instance, historical stock data might be used to inform algorithms for predicting future price movements, while sentiment analysis from social media can gauge market mood in real-time.

Yet, data by itself is only as good as the systems and processes used to manage it. Financial institutions often face the challenge of data siloing, where data is stored and processed in a decentralized manner. This can pose hurdles in creating holistic models that need a comprehensive data view. Addressing this challenge involves implementing robust data integration strategies. Data lakes and warehouses have become integral to financial operations, providing centralized repositories where data from different sources can be aggregated and made accessible for analysis.

To maximize the efficacy of deep learning models, clean and well-prepared data is essential. Data preprocessing includes steps like cleansing, normalization, and transformation. Cleansing data ensures that inaccuracies, such as duplicates or errors, are addressed, giving models a solid foundation. Normalization brings different data attributes to a common scale without distorting differences in the ranges of values. This step is crucial when employing algorithms sensitive to scale.

Furthermore, data transformation techniques like discretization or feature engineering transform raw data into formats that machine learning algorithms can easily digest. Discretization might involve converting continuous data into discrete categories, simplifying complex patterns for algorithms. Feature engineering, on the other hand, involves creating new input features that enhance the predictive power of models.

The depth of model training techniques in financial applications cannot be understated. These methods determine how effectively a model learns from data and can generalize that learning to new, unseen data. Supervised learning is a common approach, especially when reliable labeled data is available. Here, models are trained using input-output pairs, allowing them to predict outcomes based on new input data accurately.

Unsupervised learning, in contrast, operates without the guidance of labeled outputs, making it ideal for identifying hidden patterns within data. Clustering, a type of unsupervised learning, can uncover segments within financial datasets such as grouping similar investment portfolios. Dimensionality reduction, another unsupervised technique, helps simplify complex datasets while retaining their essential characteristics, improving model performance and interpretability.

The complexity of financial markets often necessitates the use of deep learning-specific models like neural networks. These models, especially deep neural networks, harness multiple layers to extract increasingly abstract features from data. One notable type, convolutional neural networks (CNNs), traditionally used in image processing, have found applications in financial time-series analysis. Their ability to detect temporal patterns and trends makes them invaluable in high-frequency trading and stock price prediction.

Training these complex models requires considerable computational power, enabled by advances in hardware such as GPUs. These processing units accelerate the training process, handling the vast computations involved in adjusting millions of model parameters. However, computational efficiency is not just about hardware advances; it relies significantly on training techniques like mini-batch gradient descent, which balances speed and accuracy in updating model parameters.

Another critical aspect of training deep learning models in finance is preventing overfitting, where a model becomes too tailored to the training data, reducing its effectiveness on new data. Techniques such as dropout, where certain nodes are randomly ignored during training, help in maintaining model generality. Regularization methods like L1 and L2 add penalty terms to the model's loss function, discouraging overly complex models and promoting simplicity.

Monitoring and evaluation of model performance are equally crucial in the deployment phase. Financial models must continuously align with market realities, which requires constant updates and refinements. Techniques for cross-validation, including k-fold and time-series specific methods like walk-forward validation, ensure robust performance across various market conditions. Such evaluations help in understanding a model's breadth and limits, guiding future improvements.

Beyond the mechanics of training, the ethical use of data and models looms large. With financial decisions carrying real-world implications, model developers must adhere to ethical guidelines ensuring fairness, transparency, and accountability in AI systems. Biased datasets can lead to skewed outcomes that might unfairly disadvantage certain groups. Therefore, establishing a feedback loop where models are not only trained but also routinely audited for biases is paramount.

In conclusion, the journey from raw data to actionable deep learning insights in finance is complex yet profoundly transformative. It involves a meticulous dance with data, requiring financial institutions to adopt sophisticated data integration, preprocessing, and model training techniques. As you look towards the future of deep learning in finance, a strong foundation in data sourcing and model training will not only demystify and streamline operations but will also enrich the strategic decision-making capabilities of the financial sector.

Chapter 15:
AI for Customer Experience

In the ever-evolving landscape of finance, delivering a seamless customer experience has become crucial, and AI is playing a pivotal role in this transformation. By leveraging data analytics, AI offers unprecedented levels of personalization, enabling financial institutions to tailor products and services to individual customer needs. This customization fosters stronger client relationships and boosts customer satisfaction. On the support front, AI-driven chatbots and virtual assistants are revolutionizing customer service by providing timely responses and resolving inquiries around the clock, effectively reducing waiting times and operational costs. These intelligent systems not only enhance user experience but also free up human resources for more complex tasks, paving the way for a more efficient and customer-centric financial industry. As AI continues to advance, its impact on customer experience will likely deepen, offering even more nuanced insights and capabilities that align with client expectations and demands.

Personalization and Customer Insights

The intersection of artificial intelligence and customer experience in finance offers a profound transformation, characterized by the burgeoning capabilities of personalization and deep customer insights. In a world overflowing with choices, financial institutions are turning to AI to deliver experiences that resonate on a deeply personal level.

Uncovering an individual's financial journey, AI can tailor interactions and services, meeting unique needs and preferences with precision previously unattainable. This isn't just about analytics; it's about translating data into genuine empathy and understanding.

Today, personalization driven by AI goes beyond simplistic recommendations. Instead, these systems dig deep, analyzing vast datasets encompassing behavior, preferences, social interactions, and even emotional cues. By utilizing machine learning algorithms, especially those honed through deep learning techniques, AI can predict customer needs with uncanny accuracy. This predictive power represents a seismic shift from reactive approaches to a more anticipatory, proactive model in customer engagement.

One of the most compelling aspects of AI integration in finance is its ability to offer hyper-personalized financial advice. Digital financial advisors, powered by sophisticated AI, can now process colossal amounts of personal financial data alongside broader economic indicators. The result? A nuanced advisory service that can adapt to the changing contours of both the individual's life and the dynamic market landscape. Whether it's retirement planning or immediate financial goals, AI ensures the advice is timely, relevant, and most importantly, personal.

Moreover, customer insights derived from AI are proving invaluable in segmenting markets more effectively. Traditional demographics like age and income are being complemented with behavioral insights. AI identifies patterns and clusters within customer data that were previously invisible to human analysts. These new, fluid segments provide a more relevant framework for targeting marketing efforts and tailoring product offerings, which enhances customer satisfaction and loyalty.

This depth of understanding also extends into enhancing customer service. Chatbots and virtual assistants, once crude in interaction, have evolved through natural language processing (NLP) capabilities. They can interpret and respond to nuanced queries, turning every customer interaction into data to further refine the personalization engine. The continuous feedback loop created by these AI systems ensures they not only meet but anticipate consumer expectations, providing a competitive edge.

The shift towards AI-driven personalization raises questions about privacy and data security that financial institutions cannot ignore. While the benefits are clear, the ethical implications of data mining and analysis are significant. It's crucial that firms employ this technology responsibly, maintaining consumer trust by implementing robust data governance and transparency practices. Customers must feel assured that their data isn't just being used intelligently, but also ethically.

Implementing these AI-driven personalization mechanisms calls for an overhaul in how financial institutions think about IT infrastructure. Systems need to be agile, scalable, and secure to handle the inflow and processing demands of big data. Integrating AI solutions seamlessly into existing operations requires strategic investments in technology and people. Building teams equipped with expertise in data science, AI, and customer experience design becomes essential to leverage these technologies effectively.

Despite the technological challenges, the potential for AI to reshape customer relationships in finance is immense. As AI systems become more adept at analyzing complex streams of data, they will become more accurate in predicting not just financial behaviors, but the human elements that drive those behaviors. This insight allows for the crafting of experiences that are not only personalized but leave customers feeling valued and understood.

Financial institutions that master the art of AI-driven personalization can redefine loyalty in the digital age. It's not just about numbers or insights—it's about creating a genuine connection.

By continually refining these connections through data-driven insights, companies can foster brand loyalty and create barriers to entry that competitors will find challenging to overcome. Such deep-rooted customer relationships invariably drive long-term growth and profitability.

In conclusion, as we navigate through the next phases of AI integration into financial services, personalization and customer insights will stand as pivotal forces shaping the future. The seamless, empathetic experiences AI can engineer are set to be the cornerstone of next-generation financial services, heralding an era where technology serves humanity's complex financial needs in ever more nuanced and meaningful ways.

AI in Customer Service and Support

In the ever-evolving landscape of finance, AI has emerged as a transformative force, particularly in customer service and support. Financial institutions are leveraging AI to enhance customer experience, streamline operations, and reduce costs. The adoption of AI technologies in customer service is driven by the demand for efficiency and the need to meet increasing customer expectations for personalized interactions.

Traditional customer service models relied heavily on human agents, which often led to long wait times and inconsistent service quality. AI, through chatbots and virtual assistants, is changing this dynamic by providing instant, 24/7 support. These AI-driven tools can handle a multitude of tasks ranging from answering frequently asked questions to assisting with complex financial transactions. By automating routine inquiries, AI allows human agents to focus on more intricate issues, thereby improving overall service quality.

An essential component of AI in customer service is natural language processing (NLP), which enables machines to understand

and respond to human language. NLP allows AI systems to interpret customer queries, extract relevant information, and provide accurate responses. This capability not only enhances the efficiency of customer interactions but also adds a level of personalization that was previously unattainable. For instance, AI can analyze a customer's past interactions and current sentiment to tailor responses that align with the individual's needs.

Moreover, AI-powered customer service tools can learn and adapt over time. Machine learning algorithms enable these systems to improve their responses based on past interactions. As a result, the more these systems are used, the more effective they become at handling complex queries and providing insightful suggestions. This adaptive learning process is a cornerstone of AI's contribution to customer support, offering a continuously evolving service model that meets the shifting demands of the financial industry.

The integration of AI into customer service also facilitates data-driven decision-making. By analyzing customer interactions, AI provides valuable insights into customer behaviors and preferences, which can be leveraged to enhance product offerings and marketing strategies. Financial institutions can use this data to predict future trends and adjust their services accordingly, ensuring they remain competitive in a rapidly changing market.

AI's role in customer service extends beyond efficiency and personalization; it's also pivotal in risk management and fraud detection. AI systems can monitor customer interactions in real-time, identifying suspicious activities and potential fraud. By analyzing patterns and anomalies in data, AI can raise alerts before any significant damage occurs. This proactive approach not only protects the financial institution but also builds trust with customers, who rely on these services to safeguard their financial interests.

It's evident that AI's impact on customer service and support is profound. However, implementing these technologies is not without challenges. Financial institutions must navigate issues related to data privacy and security. Protecting customer data is paramount, and AI systems must be designed with robust security measures to prevent unauthorized access and breaches. Additionally, there is the challenge of integrating AI into existing infrastructures. Many financial institutions operate on legacy systems that require significant upgrades to support AI technology.

Ethical considerations also play a role. As AI systems handle more customer interactions, there is a risk of perpetuating biases in decision-making processes. Ensuring that AI algorithms are fair and unbiased is crucial for maintaining customer trust and avoiding discriminatory practices. Financial institutions must prioritize transparency and accountability in their AI operations, presenting customers with clear explanations of how their data is used and the rationale behind AI-driven decisions.

Despite these challenges, the benefits of AI in customer service and support are undeniable. Financial institutions are increasingly recognizing the value of AI in streamlining operations and enhancing customer satisfaction. By effectively implementing AI, they can achieve a competitive edge, positioning themselves as leaders in a technology-driven financial landscape.

Looking forward, the role of AI in customer service will likely expand, encompassing even more sophisticated capabilities. We can expect the development of AI systems that use advanced emotional intelligence to understand and respond to customer emotions more effectively. This progression will further blur the lines between human and machine interactions, opening up new possibilities for customer engagement and satisfaction.

Ultimately, AI in customer service and support is shaping the future of finance by fostering innovation and delivering superior customer experiences. Financial institutions that embrace these technologies will not only enhance their service offerings but also secure their place in an increasingly digital world. As AI continues to advance, its integration into customer service domains will only deepen, driving ongoing transformation in how financial services are delivered and consumed.

Chapter 16:
Quantitative Finance and AI

Quantitative finance, long reliant on complex mathematical models, finds itself at the cusp of transformation through the integration of artificial intelligence. By harnessing AI's capabilities, traditional quantitative models gain unprecedented power in processing vast data sets and uncovering patterns that were once hidden. This marriage of quantitative analysis and AI facilitates a deeper understanding of market dynamics, offering a predictive edge that can significantly enhance investment strategies. As AI continues to evolve, we see a shift in how financial professionals approach data, with machine learning algorithms playing pivotal roles in optimizing portfolios and managing risk. The synergy between AI and quantitative finance holds promise for the future, where continuous learning models adapt fluidly to an ever-changing financial landscape. As the lines blur between statistical methods and intelligent algorithms, the potential for innovation in financial markets appears limitless, driving a new era of precision and performance in quantitative analysis.

Enhancing Quantitative Models with AI

In the world of quantitative finance, data reigns supreme. Quantitative analysts, often known as quants, rely on complex models and mathematical theories to analyze financial data and make predictions. Traditionally, these models have been crafted through a combination of financial theory and statistical techniques. However, with the advent of artificial intelligence, particularly machine learning, the landscape is shifting dramatically. AI is enhancing quantitative models, offering new methodologies and capabilities that redefine what's possible in financial analysis.

AI brings a powerful toolkit for enhancing model precision and predictive power. One of the key advantages is its ability to process and learn from huge datasets efficiently. While traditional models often rely on simplified assumptions and historical data, AI models can ingest a vast array of inputs, including structured data like stock prices and economic indicators as well as unstructured data sources such as news articles, social media, and even satellite images. The capacity to integrate diverse data types broadens the horizons for financial forecasting and decision-making.

Moreover, AI's learning algorithms continuously adapt to new data, allowing models to remain relevant in rapidly changing markets. Traditional models typically involve a static approach, requiring periodic recalibration based on new data. In contrast, AI models can update on-the-fly, identifying emerging patterns or anomalies in real-time. This level of adaptability is crucial in financial markets, where conditions can shift unexpectedly due to geopolitical events, regulatory changes, or technological shifts.

Machine learning techniques, such as neural networks and decision trees, are pivotal in enhancing quantitative models. Neural networks, inspired by the human brain, excel at identifying intricate patterns within complex datasets. They're particularly effective in capturing nonlinear relationships which are often present in financial data but can be elusive for traditional statistical methods. Decision trees, on the other hand, help in making classification decisions, offering transparency and interpretability in model conclusions, which can be appealing in risk management scenarios.

AI's contribution to qualitative models isn't just about data processing; it also extends to model development itself. Through a process known as automated machine learning (AutoML), AI can assist in selecting the best model architecture and hyperparameters. AutoML expands the potential for non-experts in machine learning to design sophisticated models efficiently. With these tools, quants can tap into AI's capabilities without needing deep expertise in data science, fostering innovation and exploration within finance teams.

While the benefits of AI in quantitative finance are profound, there are challenges and considerations. One major concern is overfitting—where a model becomes too tailored to historical data, adversely affecting its performance on future data. AI models, particularly those with complex architectures, are at risk of overfitting if not managed carefully. Techniques such as cross-validation, regularization, and the use of out-of-sample testing help mitigate this risk, ensuring models remain generalizable.

Another consideration is the "black box" nature of some AI models, particularly deep learning systems. These models can deliver highly accurate predictions, yet their complexity can make it difficult to interpret how results are derived. This raises challenges in understanding model behavior and in satisfying regulatory requirements for explainability in financial decisions. Emerging research in explainable AI (XAI) is beginning to address these concerns, offering methodologies to interpret AI-driven predictions and ensuring transparency.

Integration of AI into quantitative models also necessitates robust computational infrastructure. Financial institutions must invest in scalable processing power and storage solutions to manage AI workloads. Cloud computing offers a flexible and scalable option, enabling financial organizations to quickly ramp up their computational capacities. Moreover, AI development in finance requires interdisciplinary collaboration, combining expertise from finance, data science, and technology sectors to leverage AI fully.

The benefits AI brings to quantitative finance are reflected in various applications. In algorithmic trading, for instance, AI-enhanced models facilitate the development of strategies that can outperform traditional models by capturing subtle market signals and reacting to market movements with impressive speed. Similarly, AI models are used in portfolio optimization, refining asset allocation to manage risk more effectively while maximizing returns based on sophisticated predictive insights.

Predictive modeling isn't the sole avenue where AI is making an impact. AI-driven sentiment analysis is being used to gauge market sentiment from vast quantities of textual data, offering an additional layer of insight for quants. This allows financial models to incorporate not just numerical data but also qualitative insights from market discussions, thus providing a more holistic view of the market landscape.

Ethical considerations also play a critical role in the deployment of AI-enhanced quantitative models. Decisions influenced by AI can have significant real-world consequences, impacting markets and investors. It's critical to ensure that AI models are designed and used responsibly, with attention to potential biases and fairness. Ensuring ethical AI systems involves adopting stringent guidelines, performing regular audits, and establishing a governance framework to manage and monitor AI applications.

In conclusion, AI is revolutionizing quantitative finance by enhancing the capability, adaptability, and precision of financial models. This revolution is enabling greater predictive accuracy, expanding the boundaries of data analytics, and fostering innovative approaches to financial decision-making. The marriage of AI and quantitative finance holds vast potential, promising to redefine traditional paradigms and opening new possibilities in the financial industry.

The Future of Quantitative Analysis

As the financial landscape shifts with rapid technological advancements, quantitative analysis is poised for a transformation unlike any seen before. Traditionally, quants – the quantitative analysts who straddle the space between finance and data science – have relied on mathematical models honed over decades to make sense of financial markets. However, the integration of artificial intelligence (AI) into quantitative finance is turning these models on their heads, promising to deliver unprecedented levels of precision, adaptability, and insight.

AI doesn't just bring incremental changes; it revolutionizes the way data is analyzed. Machine learning algorithms, able to process and learn from vast datasets with minimal human intervention, are at the forefront of this change. They're reshaping quants' roles, transforming them from pure model developers into data curators and strategists who leverage AI to distill actionable insights. Where once a simple regression might suffice, today's AI systems can identify patterns and correlations that traditionally defy human cognition.

It's worth considering how quantitative models are being enhanced and, in some cases, completely redefined by AI. Take, for instance, the ability of neural networks, particularly deep learning models, to discern complex patterns in unstructured data. These systems can integrate non-traditional data sources – such as social media sentiment, news analytics, and satellite imagery – into quant models. This ability to process diverse data shifts the ground beneath the feet of traditional quant strategies, offering a competitive edge in predicting market movements.

However, embracing AI in quantitative analysis isn't just about adding new tools to the toolkit; it's about rethinking the foundation upon which these tools are applied. The increased complexity and opacity of AI models usher in debates about interpretability and trust. For finance professionals, understanding the mechanics behind AI-driven insights is paramount, and herein lies the challenge. As models become more intricate, they can also become a black box, making it difficult to explain decision-making processes to stakeholders.

Quants must grapple with the interplay between sophisticated AI models and the inherent risks they bring. As AI gains foothold, its ability to self-learn and adapt raises concerns about model stability and reliability, especially during market anomalies. It's crucial for finance experts to design AI systems that not only enhance predictive power but also maintain robustness against unforeseen market conditions. The future of quant analysis necessitates a balanced approach, one that blends cutting-edge AI with the intuitive understanding that seasoned analysts bring to the table.

In this evolving landscape, collaboration between disciplines becomes more critical than ever. The confluence of skills from data science, financial theory, and domain-specific knowledge is creating a new breed of quant analysts. They don't just crunch numbers; they orchestrate a symphony of data, model, and market understanding. This collaborative approach is essential to harness the full potential of AI while mitigating its risks.

The anticipated emergence of Quantum Computing represents yet another wrinkle in the future of quantitative analysis. By drastically reducing computation times and expanding problem-solving capacities, quantum technologies could further extend AI's capabilities in finance. Though widespread implementation remains over the horizon, quants are already exploring its potential impact on complex derivative pricing and optimization techniques, poised to problem-solve at scales and speeds not currently possible.

Moreover, ethical considerations can't be overlooked as AI continues to gain traction in quantitative analysis. As algorithms begin to make more decisions autonomously, there's increasing scrutiny over how these models are developed and governed. Transparency in AI's application within finance will be crucial to building trust: both in terms of regulatory compliance and ensuring that AI-driven decisions uphold fairness and objectivity.

Finally, AI in quantitative finance also has profound implications for the workforce. The traditional role of the quant is being redefined, with new roles emerging that emphasize a blend of AI acumen and financial expertise. Education systems and professional training programs will need to pivot to prepare the next generation of analysts who are not only proficient in statistical methods but also agile in AI technologies.

In conclusion, the future of quantitative analysis is bound to be characterized by versatility, powered by AI's capacity to enhance and expand the boundaries of traditional finance. As the sector embraces these advancements, the role of quantitative professionals will be increasingly dynamic, blending deep financial insight with technological proficiency. As we look to the future, the challenge and opportunity will lie in navigating this crossroads, ensuring that the promise of AI enhances the precision, reliability, and ethical grounding of quantitative finance.

Chapter 17:
Cybersecurity and AI in Finance

In an era where financial institutions are digitizing rapidly, the intersection of cybersecurity and AI has become pivotal. Financial data protection isn't just about keeping hackers at bay; it's about deploying robust AI strategies that can predict and combat cyber threats before they escalate. AI's predictive capabilities enable real-time threat detection and swift response actions, making it a cornerstone of modern cybersecurity frameworks. Sophisticated algorithms analyze vast datasets to identify anomalies and potential breaches, offering a proactive defense against ever-evolving cybercriminal tactics. Additionally, the integration of AI in cybersecurity helps reduce false positives, allowing finance professionals to focus on genuine threats rather than being overwhelmed by noise. As the financial sector continues to embrace AI, its role in fortifying cybersecurity measures offers not just protection, but also a strategic advantage in maintaining trust and resilience in an increasingly interconnected world.

Protecting Financial Data with AI

In an era where financial institutions are increasingly dependent on digital frameworks, the protection of sensitive financial data has never been more critical. With the growing sophistication of cyber threats, banks and other financial entities are leveraging artificial intelligence (AI) to bolster their cybersecurity defenses. In this section, we explore how AI is being deployed to protect financial data, ensuring not only security but also fostering trust in the digital financial ecosystem.

AI-driven solutions have transformed the cybersecurity landscape by providing proactive measures against potential threats. Unlike traditional security systems, which often function on predefined rules and patterns, AI systems adapt to evolving threats in real-time. This dynamic adaptability allows AI to identify irregularities and potential breaches far more effectively. For financial institutions dealing with massive volumes of transactions daily, AI offers a level of vigilance that human oversight simply can't match.

Machine learning, a subset of AI, plays a significant role in enhancing cybersecurity for financial data. These algorithms analyze vast datasets to learn and predict patterns associated with both legitimate and malicious activities. By continuously ingesting and analyzing data, machine learning models can identify subtle signs of cyber threats such as phishing attempts, unauthorized access, and data breaches, alerting security teams to take swift action. This real-time analysis is crucial in mitigating risks before they escalate into full-fledged cyber attacks.

Furthermore, AI helps in anomaly detection—a vital tool in guarding against data breaches. In every financial institution, certain baseline behaviors are expected within the network. Anomalies, drastic deviations from these norms, could signal a breach or an attempted intrusion. AI systems are adept at quickly identifying such anomalies amidst vast amounts of data by distinguishing between benign irregularities and those that might pose a security risk. This capability enables financial firms to respond to threats before they can cause significant harm.

Automation of threat detection and response is another area where AI shines. By automating routine surveillance and response actions, financial institutions can reduce the human error inherent in manual systems. Furthermore, AI can swiftly prioritize alerts based on the severity of potential threats, ensuring that cybersecurity teams focus their efforts where they are needed most. This efficient allocation of resources not only enhances security but also optimizes operational costs.

Another notable AI application in cybersecurity for finance is natural language processing (NLP). NLP can be used to process unstructured data, such as emails and messages, to identify phishing scams and other social engineering tactics. By scanning text for common red flags and unusual language patterns, NLP tools can determine the likelihood of fraudulent intent and thus help prevent potentially catastrophic breaches.

Conversely, AI also brings challenges that financial institutions must address. The reliance on AI and machine learning frameworks introduces complex dependencies on data accuracy and algorithmic integrity. Poor-quality data can lead to inaccurate threat assessments, while biases in machine learning models could create blind spots in security monitoring. Therefore, maintaining the precision and fairness of AI systems is imperative. Financial institutions must implement rigorous model validation processes and continuously update datasets to reflect current threat landscapes.

Ensuring transparency and explainability of AI systems is critical in building trust among stakeholders. Financial firms need to ensure that AI-driven decisions, especially those impacting security and privacy, are explainable to decision-makers and regulators. By maintaining a transparent AI framework, organizations can address privacy concerns and ensure compliance with legal norms, ultimately fostering greater confidence in their cybersecurity capabilities.

Moreover, AI enhances identity verification processes, which are crucial for protecting customer data. Using biometric data to authenticate users, such as facial recognition or fingerprint scanning, allows financial institutions to add an extra layer of verification, making unauthorized access less likely. AI systems can analyze the biometric data to verify identities with high accuracy, drastically reducing the chances of fraudulent access.

The development of adversarial AI tools that learn to bypass security measures is a potential risk. Just as AI is used to defend against cyber threats, it can be used by attackers to identify vulnerabilities and exploit them. This creates a continuous arms race between cyber attackers and defenders. To counter these adversarial threats, financial institutions must adopt an agile approach in updating their AI algorithms and strategies.

Finally, AI's role in data encryption is gaining prominence. As cyber threats become increasingly complex, traditional encryption methods are often insufficient. AI can enhance encryptions by identifying areas in data at higher risk and applying adaptive encryption techniques accordingly. This ability to evaluate risk and prioritize protection dynamically can be crucial in safeguarding sensitive financial data.

In conclusion, the application of AI in protecting financial data represents a significant advancement in cybersecurity. AI provides unparalleled tools for threat detection, risk assessment, and system automation, ultimately fortifying defenses against the continually evolving cyber threats. However, financial institutions must remain vigilant in ensuring data integrity and transparency to maximize the benefits of AI while mitigating potential risks. The dynamic interplay between AI innovation and cybersecurity in the financial sector points to a future where these technologies are not just a defense mechanism but a fundamental part of financial services infrastructure.

AI Strategies to Combat Cyber Threats

In the constantly evolving world of finance, cybersecurity has become a critical concern. The introduction of artificial intelligence (AI) into the cybersecurity domain offers significant advancements in the protection of financial data. The harmony between AI and cybersecurity heralds a future where cyber threats are not just managed, but are anticipated and proactively countered. This section explores how AI is shaping new strategies to combat cyber threats in the finance industry, ensuring the integrity and security of financial data.

AI's ability to process vast amounts of data quickly and accurately makes it an indispensable tool in identifying potential threats. Traditional cybersecurity measures, while effective to a degree, often rely on pre-established rules that can make them slow to respond to new and emerging threats. AI, on the other hand, uses machine learning algorithms that continually adapt and learn from new data. This enables financial institutions to detect anomalies and irregularities in real time, paving the way for rapid threat response and mitigation.

The role of AI in pattern recognition is particularly crucial. Financial transactions generate massive amounts of data every second, and within this influx of information, AI excels at detecting patterns that might indicate fraudulent activity or data breaches. By analyzing user behavior, transaction types, and historical data, AI systems can flag suspicious activities that deviate from the norm. This not only accelerates the identification of potential threats but also minimizes false positives, which can otherwise strain security resources and impact user trust.

Predictive analytics, powered by AI, advances the fight against cyber threats by forecasting where attackers might strike next. These systems analyze historical attack data and use sophisticated algorithms to predict future vulnerabilities. This enables financial institutions to shore up defenses in particular areas before an actual attack occurs. Predictive AI serves as a strategic advantage, allowing for resource allocation and security investments that are informed by foresight rather than hindsight.

Moreover, AI's role extends beyond merely identifying threats to actively responding to them. AI-driven response systems can autonomously take action against cyber threats by closing security gaps, quarantining affected segments, and even conducting tuning operations to prevent future breaches. This rapid and often automated response reduces the window of opportunity for cybercriminals and mitigates the potential damage of attacks.

Of course, the integration of AI into cybersecurity strategies does come with its own set of challenges. There are concerns around AI's accountability and the potential for adversarial attacks where malicious actors manipulate AI systems to bypass security controls. Financial institutions, while harnessing AI's capabilities, must remain vigilant about these potential vulnerabilities. Building robust AI systems with transparent algorithms and a strong ethical framework is essential to ensuring they strengthen rather than compromise cybersecurity protocols.

Additionally, AI can help streamline security management in multinational financial firms. By deploying AI systems across global networks, institutions can achieve consistency in security protocols and reporting. These systems provide crucial insights into regional threat landscapes, adjusting defenses based on localized intelligence while maintaining a cohesive global security posture. Such a unified approach is critical in an interconnected world where cyber threats often don't adhere to geographical boundaries.

Finally, AI empowers cybersecurity professionals by reducing the burden of mundane tasks, thereby enabling them to focus on high-level strategic efforts. Automated threat detection and response free up valuable human resources, allowing cybersecurity teams to devise more sophisticated proactive strategies and conduct thorough vulnerability assessments. It's a synergy that amplifies human capability through intelligent technology, positioning the financial sector to thwart cyber threats more effectively.

As the financial landscape continues to integrate AI, the sector must remain committed to ongoing research and development to stay ahead of cybercriminal activities. The dynamic nature of cyber threats necessitates that AI systems remain flexible and continuously updated. Collaborative efforts between financial institutions, tech firms, and regulators are essential to foster a robust ecosystem where cybersecurity through AI remains resilient and adaptive.

In conclusion, AI is not just a supplementary tool for cybersecurity in finance—it's a transformative force. By enhancing detection capabilities, enabling predictive insights, and automating responses, AI-driven strategies are reshaping how financial institutions safeguard their operations and customer data. As we move further into a digital era, leveraging AI in cybersecurity isn't just a tactical advantage; it's a necessity for survival in the modern financial landscape.

Chapter 18:
AI-Driven Financial Forecasting

Artificial intelligence is reshaping the art and science of financial forecasting, offering unprecedented accuracy and insights into market dynamics. By leveraging vast datasets and advanced algorithms, AI-driven financial forecasting tools decode complex market patterns, allowing professionals to anticipate trends with remarkable precision. This not only enhances decision-making but also mitigates risk by predicting economic shifts before they happen. In the fast-paced world of finance, where volatility is the norm, AI's predictive capabilities provide a competitive edge by swiftly adapting to changing conditions. As these technologies evolve, they enable analysts and investors to transform traditional forecasting methods, turning raw data into strategic advantages. With AI augmenting human intuition, the future of financial forecasting looks promising, offering a blend of art and algorithm that's set to redefine the industry's landscape.

Techniques in AI Financial Predictions

AI-driven financial forecasting is at the cutting edge of how markets are analyzed and understood. With an expanding toolkit of machine learning methodologies and ever-growing datasets, AI techniques shape predictions that were once merely speculative. Predictions made from AI don't just relay what's probable; they help in foreseeing the financial tides, offering investors and analysts a distinct edge in an unpredictable market environment.

At the heart of AI's predictive prowess lies the technique of *supervised learning*. It's an approach where algorithms are trained on historical data, detecting patterns and anomalies that might escape the naked eye. Such patterns help forecasters predict future performance metrics of stocks, bonds, and commodities with increasing accuracy. The capacity of these models to learn and adapt based on influxes of new data means that predictions get sharper the more they're used, transforming past trends into future insights.

But supervised learning isn't the only tool in the AI arsenal. *Unsupervised learning* stands out, especially when the data lacks clear labels or outcomes. This approach clusters and categorizes data, revealing hidden structures or correlations without any prior assumptions. In financial contexts, unsupervised techniques can illuminate obscure trends in consumer behavior or anomalies in trading patterns that traditional methods might overlook, providing insights into market sentiment or emerging financial risks.

Further enhancing predictive capabilities are **ensemble methods**. By combining multiple predictive models, these techniques offer a more nuanced and robust forecast. Methods like random forests and gradient boosting create ensembles where individual model predictions are aggregated, often resulting in a combined output that outperforms any single model's prediction. This approach mirrors the wisdom of crowds, where varied perspectives converge to form a more accurate picture of market direction.

The advent of *deep learning* has introduced neural networks capable of processing vast amounts of data through complex architectures. These neural networks are adept at recognizing intricate patterns across diverse datasets. They find utility in scenarios that involve high-dimensional data, such as predicting stock price movements based on news articles, social media sentiment, or even satellite imagery of factory outputs. Their multilayered processes mimic human cognition, allowing them to make connections that are both abstract and tangible, enhancing the depth of financial forecasts.

Another innovative technique in AI financial predictions is **recurrent neural networks (RNNs)**, particularly those using long short-term memory (LSTM) units. RNNs excel in areas where sequence or temporal data are involved - a perfect match for financial markets dictated by time-series data. LSTM networks, with their ability to remember long-term dependencies, provide profound insights by learning from sequential data inputs, continuously refining predictions as new data streams in.

In the realm of financial predictions, time is synonymous with change. Enter *reinforcement learning*—a method where models learn optimal decision-making through trial and error, akin to how one might learn to navigate a complex game. In trading, these models simulate market conditions to learn profitable strategies over time. Well-trained reinforcement models can adeptly adjust strategies in real-time, providing dynamic responses to ever-evolving market conditions, much like a seasoned trader but with the speed and precision of AI.

As the complexity and volatility of global markets persist, hybrid models that blend various AI techniques are emerging. By synthesizing the strengths of multiple approaches, hybrid models can adapt to a broader array of scenarios. Building on traditional statistical methods with AI's adaptive capabilities allows these hybrids to offer prediction results sensitive to subtle, non-linear relationships within the data, refining both precision and applicability.

Data's central role in AI predictions highlights the emerging importance of **data preprocessing techniques**. Cleaning, normalizing, and transforming raw data ensures that AI models aren't tripped by noise, outliers, or biases. In the financial domain, where inaccuracies can lead to significant monetary losses, preprocessing protects the integrity of predictions, ensuring they're grounded in reliable inputs.

With these varied techniques, the challenge isn't just technical. It's about integrating these methodologies into the decision-making fabric of financial institutions. To ensure predictions aren't just theoretically sound but practically relevant, financial professionals must often collaborate closely with data scientists, fostering a dialog between intuitive, experience-driven insights, and raw, data-oriented conclusions.

This interplay of human intuition bolstered by AI-driven insights creates a comprehensive forecasting system, markedly reducing the blind spots inherent in traditional prediction models. Increasingly, AI techniques are becoming indispensable tools, empowering investors and financial professionals to navigate markets with unprecedented acuity.

These methods have transformed financial forecasting into a dynamic landscape rich with potential. As AI techniques continuously evolve, they're set to redefine what it means to predict. The ambitions extend beyond mere accuracy—they seek to anticipate, adapt, and ultimately, steer financial currents with an intelligence that combines computational precision with strategic intuition.

With a panorama of techniques continually expanding, AI financial predictions are not just about anticipating what's next; they are about reshaping the future of finance into a field where data drives decisions and foresight becomes actionable.

Analyzing Market Trends with AI

In an ever-evolving financial landscape, the ascent of artificial intelligence in analyzing market trends represents a groundbreaking shift in investment strategies and decision-making. With AI's ability to process vast amounts of data at lightning speed, finance professionals are gaining insights that were previously unimaginable. This capacity allows them to make more informed predictions about market behaviors, be they long-term trends or short-term fluctuations.

At its core, AI's prowess in trend analysis comes from its ability to detect non-linear patterns and relationships within data sets. Traditional statistical models often struggle with the dynamic nature of financial markets, where variables constantly change. By employing machine learning algorithms, AI systems can adapt and learn from real-time data, honing predictions and enhancing overall accuracy. As a result, AI-driven insights aren't just more accurate; they're timelier, enabling more proactive approaches to capital management.

The role of AI in financial forecasting goes beyond just crunching numbers. Natural language processing (NLP), a subset of AI, is also making waves by dissecting news articles, social media posts, and financial reports to gauge public sentiment and potential market impacts. This qualitative aspect of trend analysis is crucial, as market movements can often be driven by collective sentiment and psychological triggers rather than pure fundamentals.

Moreover, AI enables the synthesis of diverse data sets, encompassing economic indicators, sector-specific news, and company performance metrics. By integrating these varied data sources, AI can provide a holistic view of market trends. This comprehensive perspective aids investors in pinpointing emerging trends before they become widely recognized, hence fostering a competitive edge.

However, the application of AI in market trend analysis isn't without its challenges. One significant hurdle is the quality of the data. AI models are only as good as the data they're trained on, making the accuracy, timeliness, and completeness of data critical elements that can affect the reliability of AI-generated forecasts. Finance professionals must ensure robust data management practices are in place to maintain the efficacy of AI applications.

In analyzing market trends, AI also plays a pivotal role in mitigating human bias. Traditional forecasting methods often grapple with subjective interpretations, influenced by the forecaster's biases or overreliance on historical data. AI, armed with sophisticated algorithms, evaluates data with greater objectivity, minimizing the likelihood of human error and enhancing the credibility of market predictions. By removing human bias, AI helps institutions and investors navigate complex market landscapes with greater confidence.

The use of AI to spot trends isn't just confined to traditional asset classes like stocks and bonds. It's also revolutionizing how various financial instruments are evaluated, including derivatives, options, and cryptocurrencies. Each of these markets presents unique challenges and opportunities, and AI's advanced analytical capabilities are indispensable in staying ahead of their rapidly changing dynamics.

Furthermore, as AI becomes more ingrained in analyzing market trends, finance professionals are excited about the possibilities of predictive analytics. This forward-looking approach doesn't just analyze what has happened but anticipates future scenarios. By leveraging AI's analytical capacity, financial institutions can model potential future outcomes, enabling better strategic planning and risk management.

Another intriguing application of AI in market trend analysis is the identification of market anomalies. Markets aren't always rational, often influenced by unexpected geopolitical events, regulatory changes, or significant industry disruptions. AI systems can quickly detect deviations from normal market patterns, alerting finance professionals to underlying factors that might not be immediately apparent through conventional analysis.

The integration of AI in market trend analysis also brings up ethical considerations. As AI becomes more autonomous, ensuring that decision-making processes remain transparent and aligned with ethical standards is paramount. Finance professionals must balance leveraging AI's capabilities with the responsibility of maintaining market integrity and consumer trust.

Despite the challenges, the synergy between AI and market trend analysis is invaluable. It empowers financial professionals to navigate the volatility of today's markets with a level of insight that is both deep and nuanced. As AI technologies continue to advance, their impact on financial forecasting and market trend analysis will undoubtedly expand, offering even more sophisticated tools to interpret and respond to the complexities of global finance.

The future of market trend analysis with AI is bright, with endless possibilities on the horizon. As AI continues to evolve, its applications in financial markets are expected to deepen, becoming more sophisticated and integrative. From enhanced predictive capabilities to more complex behavioral pattern analyses, AI is set to redefine how market trends are identified and leveraged, guiding the financial industry into a new era of innovation and progress.

Chapter 19:
Innovation and Startup Ecosystem

The financial sector is witnessing a surge in innovation, primarily driven by a vibrant startup ecosystem leveraging the potential of artificial intelligence. This dynamic space is rich with opportunities for collaboration between nimble startups and established financial institutions, creating a fertile ground for revolutionary AI applications. Startups, unfettered by legacy systems, are agile and can swiftly adopt cutting-edge AI technologies, offering novel solutions in areas ranging from investment advice to risk analysis. Their innovations often spark a ripple effect, challenging traditional players to innovate or partner to stay competitive. Through incubators, accelerators, and strategic alliances, financial institutions and startups are forging partnerships that not only bring fresh perspectives to the industry but also accelerate the adoption of AI-driven solutions in finance. Such synergies enable both parties to harness each other's strengths, driving a transformative change in how financial services are delivered, ultimately reshaping the future landscape for investors, consumers, and businesses alike.

How Startups Are Leveraging AI

In the rapidly evolving landscape of finance, startups are playing a pivotal role in harnessing the power of artificial intelligence (AI) to catalyze innovation. They are not just adapting to the changing environment but actively shaping it, using AI to transform traditional paradigms and explore uncharted territories. This section explores the myriad ways in which startups are leveraging AI to make significant strides in the financial industry.

One of the most impactful areas where startups are applying AI is in data analytics. By capturing and analyzing vast amounts of data, AI-powered startups are offering novel insights that were previously out of reach. These insights aren't just improving decision-making processes; they're redefining them. For instance, companies like *Stripe* and *Plaid* are utilizing AI to process transactions safely while maintaining an extraordinary level of efficiency. This has not only streamlined payment processes but also enhanced the customer experience by making transactions more reliable and faster.

AI-driven startups are also making significant inroads into the realm of investment management. Through machine learning algorithms, they create bespoke investment strategies tailored to individual risk profiles and goals. This level of customization was unthinkable with traditional methods due to its complexity and resource demands. Startups like *Betterment* and *Wealthfront* have pioneered the use of robo-advisors, which leverage AI to offer accessible wealth management services to a broader audience, democratizing investment opportunities.

Another critical area of application is in fraud detection and risk management. Startups recognize that AI's capacity for pattern recognition and anomaly detection surpasses human capabilities. Companies such as *Feedzai* and *Darktrace* innovate by deploying AI systems that monitor large numbers of transactions in real-time, providing alerts for suspicious activities. These systems can predict and preempt fraud attempts, thus mitigating risks long before they manifest.

Moreover, the AI capabilities found in startups extend into enhancing customer service through natural language processing

(NLP). By integrating AI chatbots and virtual assistants into their operations, startups are providing faster, more efficient customer service solutions that can handle queries at any time. Startups like *Kasisto*, which develops conversational AI for financial institutions, enable customers to access information and make informed decisions without needing human intervention, thus significantly reducing wait times and operational costs.

The integration of AI into fintech has also opened new frontiers in credit scoring and lending. Startups are crafting innovative credit assessment models that incorporate non-traditional datasets, such as social media activity and utility payments. This approach, leading the charge for holistic credit assessments, ensures that creditworthy individuals who might have been overlooked by conventional models get their fair evaluation. Products from firms like *Upstart* and *Zest AI* have shown how AI can reduce poverty and financial inequality by providing credit access to underserved populations.

Fintech startups are not just leveraging AI for financial gains; they are also using it to foster collaboration within the financial ecosystem. Through partnerships with larger financial institutions, startups bring agility and innovation, while the incumbents offer scale and resources. This collaborative ecosystem benefits all parties involved, including most importantly, the end-users, who enjoy more refined and efficient services. Examples of such synergistic partnerships include accelerators and innovation labs developed by traditional banks in collaboration with AI-focused startups, such as JP Morgan's collaboration with AI startups through its In-Residence program.

The entrepreneurial spirit driving startups also ties into the ethics and responsibilities associated with deploying AI in financial services. Recognizing the potential risks, these innovators are often at the forefront of advocating for ethical AI deployment and developing frameworks to ensure transparency and fairness. The rise of responsible AI startups shows a commitment to not only leverage AI for economic gains but also to build trust and integrity within the financial system.

AI's role doesn't stop at current technologies but is constantly evolving, with startups continuously pushing the boundaries of what's possible. Advances in quantum computing, for instance, promise to further accelerate AI capabilities. Startups that are early adopters of such technologies could potentially unlock unprecedented processing power, thereby opening another realm of possibilities in financial forecasting and risk management.

As we integrate increasingly sophisticated AI tools, the inherent disruption leads to the redefinition of roles within startups. AI doesn't just enhance existing jobs; it creates new roles and necessitates a continuous upskilling of the workforce. This dynamic environment fosters a culture of constant learning and adaptability—hallmarks of successful startups operating at the fringe of technological advancement.

To conclude, the nimbleness of startups allows them to explore and implement AI technologies with agility and creativity that larger institutions might struggle to match. By adopting a bold and innovative approach, startups are redefining the financial landscape, creating smart solutions, and aligning tightly with the future of financial services. As AI continues to advance, its role in supporting and driving the success of startups will likely become even more pronounced, signaling a transformative era in finance where innovation knows no bounds.

Collaboration between Startups and Financial Institutions

The financial industry, historically characterized by established institutions and traditional practices, is undergoing a rapid transformation. Central to this evolution is the collaboration between startups and financial institutions. While financial institutions bring experience, regulatory knowledge, and extensive customer bases, startups inject agility, innovation, and cutting-edge technology into the equation.

Startups serve as the catalyst for change, challenging long-standing industry norms and introducing innovative solutions. Their smaller size allows them to pivot quickly and experiment with AI-driven technologies without the bureaucratic constraints that often impede larger organizations. This flexibility is paramount in a world where technological advancements are frequent and disruptive.

Financial institutions, on the other hand, provide a robust infrastructure. They possess the resources and capabilities to support large-scale deployments of new technologies but often lack the innovative spark needed to develop solutions from scratch. By partnering with startups, these institutions can access niche technologies and integrate them into their existing frameworks, effectively bridging the gap between tradition and innovation.

This mutually beneficial relationship is evident in the realm of artificial intelligence, where startups are pioneering technologies like machine learning algorithms, natural language processing, and blockchain solutions. By collaborating with startups, financial institutions can leverage these technologies to enhance their services, improve operational efficiency, and better manage risks. Such partnerships enable financial institutions to offer personalized customer experiences while maintaining the stringent security and compliance standards critical to the industry.

Nevertheless, collaboration is not without its challenges. Cultural differences between startups and established financial entities can lead to friction. Startups operate in environments that prioritize innovation and rapid change, whereas financial institutions are often more risk-averse, focusing on compliance and stability. Successful partnerships require aligning these divergent perspectives and finding a middle ground that respects both agility and prudence.

Furthermore, regulatory complexities pose significant hurdles. Financial institutions are governed by strict regulations designed to protect consumers and maintain financial stability. Startups, lacking experience in navigating this intricate regulatory landscape, may find it daunting. Effective collaboration necessitates startups gaining a thorough understanding of these regulations and financial institutions providing guidance to ensure compliance.

Despite these challenges, the synergies between startups and financial institutions are compelling. Startups can help financial institutions respond to the increasing demand for digital transformation and innovation from consumers, who are now accustomed to seamless digital experiences in other areas of their lives. Through these collaborations, financial institutions can expand their digital capabilities without the need for developing in-house solutions, which can be costly and time-consuming.

The fintech sector serves as a primary example of successful collaboration. Here, partnerships have led to groundbreaking solutions in areas like mobile payments, lending platforms, and wealth management. The integration of AI-driven technologies in these areas has not only increased efficiency but also enhanced the user experience by providing faster, more accurate services.

Strategic partnerships also facilitate faster market entry for startups. By leveraging the established brand and customer trust of financial institutions, startups can overcome entry barriers and scale their innovations more quickly. This collaboration is especially beneficial in regions where regulatory approval can be a lengthy and cumbersome process.

Many financial institutions have recognized these advantages, leading to the creation of innovation labs, accelerators, and venture funds specifically designed to nurture relationships with startups. These initiatives provide startups with resources, mentorship, and access to funding, allowing them to innovate while staying aligned with the strategic goals of their financial partners.

There are numerous case studies highlighting the success of such collaborations. For instance, large banks have partnered with AI startups to create sophisticated algorithmic trading platforms that can process vast amounts of data at high speed and accuracy. These platforms are revolutionizing how purchasing decisions are made, ultimately enhancing the banks' investment strategies.

Moreover, the collaboration is opening new avenues for ethical AI development. Working with startups committed to ethical AI can help financial institutions build systems that are transparent and fair, addressing concerns about bias and privacy. This is particularly relevant in areas like credit scoring, where AI can help refine decision-making processes to be more inclusive and equitable.

In conclusion, the collaboration between startups and financial institutions is reshaping the financial landscape. By combining their respective strengths, these partners can drive innovation while managing the complexities of the modern financial ecosystem. The symbiotic relationship not only accelerates the adoption of AI technologies but also ensures that the industry remains responsive to dynamic market needs and regulatory frameworks. As these partnerships evolve, they hold the promise of a more agile, customer-centric financial sector primed for future challenges. Ultimately, this collaboration represents a strategic opportunity to blend creativity with stability, paving the way for next-generation financial services.

Chapter 20:
Infrastructure for AI in Finance

As AI becomes a cornerstone of finance, laying a robust infrastructure is crucial. Financial institutions are grappling with the dual need to modernize legacy systems while integrating new technologies. The infrastructure supporting AI should be scalable, enabling everything from data storage to processing power that meets AI's demanding requirements. Cloud computing offers a dynamic solution, providing flexibility and cost-effectiveness, but issues around data security and compliance must be addressed. In parallel, there's an urgent call for the integration of AI-ready platforms that can handle complex algorithms and real-time data analysis. As these systems evolve, firms face challenges such as ensuring interoperability with existing architectures and maintaining data integrity across multifaceted processes. Bridging these technological divides is not only a technical challenge but also a strategic necessity for financial institutions aiming to harness AI's full potential. Building AI-ready financial systems requires a visionary approach combining innovation, adaptability, and robust security frameworks, setting the stage for a future where AI's capabilities can be fully leveraged in transforming finance.

Building AI-Ready Financial Systems

The evolution of artificial intelligence (AI) in finance is undeniable. As financial institutions race to harness AI's potential, the infrastructure that supports these technologies becomes critical. Building AI-ready financial systems involves more than just incorporating advanced algorithms; it requires a holistic approach that considers data integration, computational power, and regulatory compliance.

The first challenge is data. AI systems thrive on data, but not all data is equal, and the financial industry deals with vast amounts of unstructured data. Structured data from traditional financial statements needs to be complemented with insights extracted from news articles, social media, and global events. Ensuring the seamless integration of these diverse data types is crucial. This involves setting up robust data pipelines and storage solutions that can handle terabytes, if not petabytes, of information efficiently.

Once the data is appropriately curated, the focus shifts to computational power. Processing significant volumes of data requires substantial computational resources. Financial institutions are now leaning towards cloud-based solutions for their scalability and cost-effectiveness. The cloud offers the flexibility to rapidly scale operations without the need for upfront investments in infrastructure. Yet, not all firms are comfortable with this model due to security concerns. Thus, hybrid solutions, which balance the benefits of cloud computing while maintaining critical data on-premises, are gaining traction.

Security is another indispensable element. As financial institutions deploy AI systems, securing sensitive financial data becomes paramount. The architecture of these systems needs to include robust cybersecurity measures. Using AI-driven techniques to identify and mitigate threats can be seen as both a necessity and an advantage. However, it's a double-edged sword; just as AI can bolster defenses, it's also being used by adversaries to craft sophisticated attacks.

Ensuring interoperability between various systems and platforms is also vital. Financial institutions often deal with legacy systems that weren't designed to work with modern AI technologies. The inability to communicate seamlessly between these systems can create bottlenecks. To address this, building flexible systems with open APIs becomes a strategic priority. This way, new technologies can be effectively integrated, allowing for smooth data flow across platforms.

Another layer to consider is regulatory compliance. Financial AI systems are subject to stringent regulations that vary across regions. These systems need to be architected to automatically track and document decisions made by AI algorithms. This "explainability" is crucial for maintaining transparency and trust. Regular audits and updates to these systems are necessary to ensure they remain compliant with evolving regulations.

The human element cannot be overlooked. Building AI-ready systems isn't just about technology; it also involves cultivating a workforce equipped to manage these advanced tools. This requires ongoing investment in training and development to keep employees up-to-date with the latest AI trends and tools. Financial institutions are also encouraged to foster a culture of innovation, where teams are empowered to experiment and iterate rapidly.

Partnerships between the finance sector and technology companies play a critical role in this transformation. Collaborations can expedite the development of these infrastructures by providing access to expertise, technology, and markets that might be otherwise inaccessible. These partnerships can also bring fresh perspectives, fostering innovation and enabling financial institutions to leapfrog into the future.

Performance measurement is an integral part of maintaining AI-ready systems. Institutions need metrics that are not just about measuring technological performance but also about understanding business impact. This means assessing how AI is contributing to revenue growth, cost savings, and customer satisfaction. Regular performance reviews ensure systems remain aligned with strategic objectives and can adapt to changing market conditions.

In conclusion, building AI-ready financial systems is a complex yet rewarding endeavor. By focusing on data integration, computational resources, security, interoperability, compliance, workforce readiness, partnerships, and performance measurement, financial institutions can ensure that they are well-positioned to leverage the full potential of AI. As these systems come online, they don't just enhance operational efficiencies; they fundamentally transform how financial services are delivered in the digital age.

Challenges in Technology Integration

As artificial intelligence continues to reshape the landscape of finance, the integration of technological infrastructure to support this evolution presents a host of challenges. Financial institutions are tasked with building robust AI-ready systems that can securely process vast sums of data and provide real-time insights. This process is fraught with complexities, not least because of existing legacy systems that many financial institutions continue to rely upon. Legacy systems often lack the flexibility to adapt rapidly to new technological demands, posing a significant hurdle in AI integration.

A critical challenge in technology integration is ensuring data compatibility across different systems. Financial institutions often gather data from various sources, each with unique formats and structures. Integrating AI effectively means normalizing this data so that it can be processed uniformly by AI algorithms. This need for data harmonization necessitates sophisticated data management systems and infrastructure, which can be both costly and resource-intensive. For institutions, the investment in transforming these systems isn't just about financial expenditure. It requires a strategic overhaul, fostering a culture that prioritizes data integrity and accessibility.

Moreover, the speed and efficiency of data processing are prerequisites for effective AI implementation. With financial markets moving at a breakneck pace, any delay in processing can result in significant losses. AI algorithms and models require not only clean data but also a high-throughput, low-latency environment to function optimally. This requirement often necessitates upgrading existing IT infrastructure, including servers and networks, to support these demands. As a result, institutions face challenges in aligning their high-speed processing capabilities with their strategic AI goals.

Security is another formidable challenge. AI systems are vulnerable to both traditional cybersecurity threats and those arising from new, sophisticated attacks aimed at exploiting AI environments. Protecting sensitive financial data—which AI relies on for decision-making—needs top-tier security measures. Financial organizations must ensure that their infrastructures are hardened against breaches while still enabling the seamless operation of AI technologies. Ensuring that suitable security protocols are in place is a constant race against evolving cyber threats.

Compliance and regulation form another layer of complexity. Integrating AI technologies in finance means navigating a labyrinthine regulatory landscape, with regulations evolving to keep pace with technological advancements. Compliance isn't just about following existing rules; it's also about forecasting future regulatory changes and constructing systems that remain adaptable. Financial institutions must align their AI systems with both domestic and international regulations, which can vary significantly between jurisdictions.

Scalability poses its set of challenges. As financial organizations grow and markets evolve, AI systems must be able to scale efficiently to manage increased data loads and more complex algorithms. Scaling AI infrastructure is more than simply adding more computing power; it involves reconfiguring systems to ensure efficiency across various components, from data storage to computational processing, which can demand considerable planning and coordination.

Cultural and organizational shifts are essential to meet these integration challenges. Adopting AI-induced changes in financial operations often meets resistance within institutions. Employees accustomed to traditional methods may view AI as a threat rather than an enabler. Changing this mindset requires robust change management strategies, decisive leadership, and training programs that equip the workforce to understand and leverage AI technologies.

The trajectory of AI integration in finance points toward an ever-deeper intertwining of technology and financial operations. Despite the technical and organizational challenges, the potential benefits of AI—improved risk management, enhanced customer service, and more dynamic investment strategies—underscore the importance of overcoming these hurdles. As technology continues to advance, so too must the strategies employed by financial institutions to integrate AI incrementally and effectively. Navigating this complex path calls for foresight, flexibility, and a willingness to innovate, ensuring that the financial sector can fully exploit the potential AI has to offer.

Chapter 21:
The Global Impact of AI in Finance

AI's intersection with finance extends beyond regional boundaries, fostering a wave of unprecedented global change. Due to differing levels of technological advancement and regulatory frameworks, the adoption of AI in finance markets varies considerably across the world. In developed economies, AI's integration into financial systems enhances efficiency, accuracy, and security, catalyzing economic growth and improved market dynamics. Emerging markets, meanwhile, grapple with infrastructural and knowledge-based challenges but see AI as a promising avenue for catching up with global financial leaders. This dynamic/global relationship fosters a complex web of cross-border opportunities and challenges, compelling financial institutions to collaborate and innovate within international coalitions. As companies navigate these intricate landscapes, the potential for AI to level financial inequalities grows, though distinct issues like data privacy, cultural variance, and regulatory divergence remain key hurdles. By recognizing these global patterns, finance professionals are better equipped to harness AI's transformative power, keeping a keen eye on ethical practices and sustainable advancements while building a resilient future for global finance.

Comparing AI Adoption Across Markets

Artificial intelligence (AI) is revolutionizing industries across the globe, and the financial sector is no exception. Yet, as with any sweeping innovation, the uptake and integration of AI in finance varies significantly from one market to another. This disparity can be attributed to factors such as the level of technological infrastructure, regulatory environments, and cultural attitudes towards AI adoption.

In developed markets like the United States and the European Union, the adoption of AI in finance is rapidly advancing. These regions benefit from robust technological infrastructures that support sophisticated AI applications. Major financial institutions in these markets are increasingly leveraging AI for tasks such as algorithmic trading, risk management, and customer service. The drive for competitive advantage and efficiency gains propels these companies to be at the forefront of AI innovation.

Meanwhile, in developing markets, AI adoption in finance is less uniform. While some countries, such as China and India, are making significant strides, others face challenges due to limited resources and infrastructure. China, in particular, presents an intriguing case with its ambitious AI initiatives supported by government policies and vast data availability. Chinese financial firms are integrating AI in everything from digital payments to credit scoring, creating a dynamic and rapidly evolving FinTech landscape.

In contrast, regions like Sub-Saharan Africa and Latin America show a varied picture. In Africa, the penetration of AI technologies lags behind due to infrastructural constraints and financial resources limitations. Yet, there's momentum in harnessing AI to increase financial inclusion through mobile banking and credit scoring for underbanked populations. Similarly, in Latin America, the primary drivers of AI in finance are startups and large technology companies entering the financial arena to offer innovative solutions tailored to local needs.

Beyond infrastructure, regulatory environments also play a critical role in shaping AI adoption in finance. In the European Union, stringent data protection laws such as the General Data Protection Regulation (GDPR) pose challenges to extensive AI deployment due to privacy concerns. However, they also push for responsible AI development, focusing on transparency, fairness, and trustworthiness. By contrast, the regulatory landscape in the Asia-Pacific region is more varied, encompassing both supportive policies and stringent restrictions, which either accelerate or hinder AI growth in finance.

The cultural context further influences AI adoption rates. In societies where there is a high level of trust in technology, such as in Nordic countries, the adoption of AI-based financial solutions faces fewer barriers. These cultures tend to be early adopters and exhibit a more open attitude towards disruptive technologies. On the other hand, regions with a skeptical view on technology, possibly due to past economic disruptions or fraud incidents, might exhibit resistance, slowing down AI penetration.

While differences exist between markets, several common trends are emerging. Universally, financial institutions are recognizing the power of AI to enhance customer experience, reduce operational costs, and provide strategic insights through data analysis. Through collaboration with technology firms and investment in AI talent, financial institutions across markets are building capabilities to harness AI.

Moreover, global standardization efforts are underway, attempting to bridge the gap between diverse regulatory frameworks and promote best practices in AI adoption. International organizations like the Financial Stability Board (FSB) and the International Organization of Securities Commissions (IOSCO) are working on harmonizing AI regulations to support cross-border financial activities.

In smaller economies, where financial ecosystems are not as mature, AI is often being used to leapfrog traditional banking systems entirely. Mobile technology and AI are paving the way for innovative financial solutions. For instance, mobile payment systems combining AI analytics have become a cornerstone for residents to access reliable financial services without needing a conventional banking infrastructure.

AI's footprint in the global financial landscape continues to expand. However, as the technology evolves, so does the complexity of managing its adoption effectively across different markets. Differences in data sources, local needs, and compliance models mean that a one-size-fits-all approach to AI integration is far from viable.

In conclusion, while AI adoption across financial markets varies, the shared goal remains to enhance financial services through technological advancement. The competitive edge that AI offers cannot be overlooked, driving financial institutions worldwide to adapt and innovate continuously. Moving forward, the challenge will be to balance the pace of AI integration with ethical, environmental, and societal considerations, ensuring inclusive benefits across diverse markets.

Cross-Border Challenges and Opportunities

The financial industry has always operated on a global scale, with money and investments flowing seamlessly across borders. With the advent of artificial intelligence (AI), the speed and complexity of these transactions have increased dramatically. However, this global reach comes with its own set of challenges and opportunities, especially in terms of regulatory environments and operational practices.

One significant challenge AI faces in a cross-border context is the lack of uniform regulations. Different countries have their own rules governing financial activities and the use of AI in such operations. This regulatory patchwork can be a stumbling block for financial institutions that wish to operate globally. They must navigate complex regulatory landscapes while ensuring compliance in multiple jurisdictions, which can increase both costs and risks. The opportunity, however, lies in creating standardized frameworks that facilitate cross-border AI operations while adhering to regional laws.

Moreover, data privacy regulations like the European Union's General Data Protection Regulation (GDPR) add another layer of complexity. Financial institutions deploying AI tools need access to vast amounts of data, often from different geographical regions. Ensuring data sharing complies with local privacy laws can be a daunting task. Yet, these challenges also present opportunities for developing sophisticated AI systems capable of securely managing and processing data in compliance with international standards, thus strengthening trust and enabling more seamless cross-border operations.

Currency fluctuations also present a unique challenge for cross-border AI applications. AI tools can analyze exchange rates and predict movements, but no model can eliminate the inherent uncertainties of the forex market completely. Institutions trading in multiple currencies must consider how AI can aid in designing effective hedging strategies to mitigate risks. Here, the opportunity lies in AI's ability to analyze vast datasets for deeper insights, improving decision-making and profit margins in volatile markets.

The cultural nuances can't be overlooked either. AI systems must be sensitive to the cultural and market differences across regions. A trading strategy or customer service AI that works well in one country may fail spectacularly in another simply due to differing consumer behaviors or market norms. Here, companies can leverage AI not only for broad analysis but also for tailoring services to different cultural and market environments, tapping into local expertise and datasets to customize their offerings effectively.

Language barriers also present hefty obstacles in cross-border AI transactions. While natural language processing has advanced significantly, the subtleties and idioms of different languages can still pose issues. Misinterpretations can lead to costly mistakes, especially in investment strategies or customer interactions. The opportunity lies in enhancing language models to better understand and process multiple languages accurately, allowing for more precise cross-border communications and transactions.

Cross-border AI investments also face infrastructure disparities. Not all countries have the same level of technological advancement or data availability, which can hinder AI operations. Financial institutions must assess local technological capabilities and adapt their AI solutions accordingly. Investments in infrastructure can also serve as opportunities for growth, enabling local economies to develop and better integrate with global financial systems.

However, deploying AI across borders also opens the door to unprecedented financial innovations. AI facilitates the connection of disparate markets, fostering more cohesive global trading systems. This integration can reduce inefficiencies, bringing unprecedented liquidity and price discovery to global markets. Financial institutions leveraging AI solutions can benefit significantly by tapping into new markets and customer bases, diversifying their revenue streams.

One of the greatest opportunities for AI lies in fintech collaborations across countries. Startups and established firms can innovate novel solutions that cater to regional markets, offering new financial products and services. These collaborations can drive economic growth, especially when companies leverage AI to solve specific regional problems, such as increasing financial inclusion or efficiently managing remittances.

Cross-border AI applications also face technical challenges related to interoperability. Different countries often use different technical standards and protocols, so ensuring AI systems can communicate and operate seamlessly is crucial. The opportunity here lies in the development of interoperability standards that permit seamless operation across borders, enabling smoother transactions and collaboration.

Despite the challenges, the use of AI in cross-border finance also opens new streams of value creation. Sophisticated AI algorithms can analyze global market data to predict trends, identify opportunities, and offer personalized advice across borders. For instance, robo-advisors using AI could give investment recommendations tailored to the global market dynamics and individual preferences, revolutionizing investment strategies, and offering competitive advantages to institutions that can effectively deploy these technologies.

Finally, the competitive landscape in AI-driven finance requires a rethinking of traditional business models. Companies must balance local expertise with global capabilities, investing in local knowledge to make better sense of global trends. This presents an opportunity for businesses to not only innovate but to disrupt traditional financial models, enabling more inclusive and efficient global markets.

In conclusion, while the cross-border application of AI in finance presents several challenges, it equally offers remarkable opportunities for growth, innovation, and enhanced global connectivity. By navigating these complexities skillfully, financial institutions can harness AI to redefine global financial landscapes, overcome regulatory hurdles, and innovate radically for better and more inclusive international financial ecosystems.

Chapter 22:
Future Trends in Financial AI

The horizon of financial AI is brimming with innovations that promise to reshape how finance professionals approach their craft. As AI technologies evolve, they are poised to integrate cutting-edge advancements like quantum computing and advanced machine learning frameworks, which could drastically reduce computational limits and improve decision-making. Simultaneously, the rise of decentralized finance (DeFi) platforms highlights a trend towards more democratized financial ecosystems, potentially altering traditional banking landscapes. Moreover, the convergence of AI with these nascent technologies could usher in unprecedented automation and personalization in financial services, offering tailored solutions that address individual needs with precision. Financial institutions must start preparing now by investing in agile infrastructures and continuous learning programs to capitalize on these transformations and remain relevant in an ever-changing digital economy. The fusion of AI with these emerging trends not only suggests a transformative future for industry insiders but also beckons a reimagining of financial interactions at every level.

Emerging Technologies to Watch

As the landscape of financial AI continues to evolve, several emerging technologies promise to reshape the industry further. Financiers and investors are becoming increasingly aware of the potential these innovations hold in transforming everything from investment strategies to risk management. This section delves into some of the most significant technological advancements on the horizon, offering insight into their possible impact on the future of finance.

Quantum computing is perhaps one of the most talked-about emerging technologies with the potential to revolutionize financial AI. This advanced computing power could process and analyze complex datasets at unprecedented speeds, dwarfing the capabilities of classical computers. As a result, the finance industry might see significant improvements in areas such as portfolio optimization, pricing of complex derivatives, and risk assessment. Quantum algorithms could enable financial institutions to model and predict market behaviors with a level of accuracy and detail that is currently beyond reach.

Another technology that's gaining traction is edge computing. While cloud computing has been the backbone for many AI applications, edge computing brings data processing closer to the source of data generation. This shift can reduce latency, enhance security, and increase the efficiency of data-driven applications. For financial entities dealing with real-time data, such as stock exchanges or high-frequency traders, this could mean faster trade execution times, improved fraud detection, and seamless customer interactions without delays.

In parallel, AI's increasingly sophisticated capabilities are being supercharged by advancements in neuromorphic computing. Inspired by the human brain, neuromorphic systems leverage specialized hardware to improve the efficiency of computations in machine learning models. This technology could drastically reduce the power consumption of data centers, thereby lowering operational costs for financial institutions that implement AI on a large scale. Neuromorphic chips can accelerate the speed and efficiency of machine learning algorithms used in trading, risk management, and customer service.

The growing importance of decentralized finance (DeFi) illustrates the dynamic nature of the financial industry. Built on blockchain technology, DeFi represents a radical shift towards more transparent, accessible, and efficient financial systems. Integrating AI into this space could lead to innovative financial products and services that are structured around smart contracts instead of traditional intermediaries. The automation potential here is enormous, ranging from loan origination to complex derivatives trading, making traditional financial operations not only more efficient but also more accessible to a wider audience.

Digital identity verification has become a cornerstone of secure financial transactions. Several emerging AI technologies are enhancing these processes with biometric recognition and blockchain integration. The synergy between AI and biometric data allows financial companies to authenticate users with greater accuracy and less friction, enhancing the security of online transactions. Furthermore, blockchain-based digital identities can securely store user data, giving users more control over their personal information while maintaining confidentiality and consent.

As AI continues to revolutionize customer experiences in finance, conversational AI is an area that's rapidly evolving. These AI systems, which include chatbots and virtual assistants, are becoming more proficient in understanding and generating human language. They can provide personalized financial advice, handle customer queries in real-time, and process various transactional services without human intervention. This advancement not only enhances customer satisfaction but also reduces operational costs for financial firms by automating routine tasks.

Finally, the Internet of Things (IoT) is creating a new frontier for AI applications in finance. With the proliferation of connected devices, there is an enormous amount of real-time data that financial firms can harness. IoT data can be used to assess risk more accurately in insurance, monitor and manage physical assets in real-time, and even influence market sentiment analysis, giving financial analysts new dimensions of data to consider in their predictions and strategies.

In conclusion, these emerging technologies are shaping a future where financial AI is more powerful, efficient, and accessible than ever before. While challenges in integration, regulation, and ethical considerations exist, the potential benefits they bring are undeniable. Financial professionals, tech enthusiasts, and investors who stay informed about these trends are likely to be better prepared to capitalize on the opportunities they present, paving the way for a more innovative and inclusive financial industry.

Preparing for a Transformative Future

As we look toward the horizon of financial technology, the fusion of artificial intelligence with the financial ecosystem invites both exhilarating advances and complex challenges. Financial institutions, startups, and investors are preparing for a future where AI not only enhances but significantly reshapes industry landscapes. This transformation requires a proactive approach to innovation adoption, organizational restructuring, and continuous learning to keep pace with rapid technological evolution.

To prepare for this transformative future, finance professionals must cultivate an understanding that AI is not just a tool but a fundamental shift in how business is conducted. It's about leveraging enormous computational power and advanced algorithms to recognize patterns, predict outcomes, and automate decisions. These capabilities can be applied to diverse areas such as customer service, trading, risk assessment, and regulatory compliance. Financial entities are leveraging AI to optimize processes, increase operational efficiency, and open new revenue streams.

A critical area of preparation involves infrastructure adaptation. Existing systems and processes will need to be realigned to integrate AI technologies effectively. This means investing in cloud computing, enhancing data storage capacities, and ensuring robust cybersecurity measures are in place. As financial transactions become increasingly digital, ensuring the security and integrity of data becomes paramount. Organizations need to develop and implement strong data governance practices to maintain client trust and ensure regulatory compliance.

Moreover, the synergy between AI and finance encourages the development of new business models. Financial institutions must be agile and willing to redefine their service offerings by embracing innovations born out of AI. This involves moving away from traditional banking models and venturing into dynamic and flexible financial services built around AI-driven insights. Personalized banking experiences tailored to individual consumer preferences and predictive product offerings can drive customer engagement and loyalty.

An often overlooked but vital aspect of preparing for a future shaped by AI is the human element. As automation and AI continue to permeate the finance sector, the roles of finance professionals are expected to evolve. There will be a greater demand for individuals who possess not only financial acumen but also technical skills in AI and machine learning. Upskilling and reskilling the workforce is essential to equip employees with the competencies required to interact with AI systems and interpret AI-generated insights.

Beyond skill development, cultivating a culture of innovation within organizations will be crucial. Encouraging experimentation and allowing for iterative learning processes will foster an environment where new ideas are tested and refined. A culture that embraces failure as a step toward innovation will be more adept at capitalizing on AI's potential. Leadership must support this cultural shift, ensuring teams are motivated and empowered to explore AI-driven solutions without the constraints of traditional limitations.

Additionally, collaboration and partnership between financial institutions and tech companies, including startups, are becoming increasingly essential. The complexity of AI technologies often requires specialized expertise that financial institutions may not possess in-house. Through partnerships, these institutions can access cutting-edge technologies and insights, accelerating their AI adoption while leveraging external innovation. Collaborative ecosystems can expand the boundaries of what's possible, offering platforms for shared learning and co-creation.

The regulatory landscape for AI in finance is another area that demands attention. As AI becomes more entrenched in financial services, regulatory frameworks will need to evolve accordingly. Financial institutions must engage with regulators to ensure that AI applications are developed and deployed ethically and transparently. Proactive collaboration with regulatory bodies can lead to the creation of policies that safeguard against AI's potential biases and risks while promoting innovation responsibly.

In the realm of ethical AI, developing fair and transparent algorithms is essential. Financial services must actively work to identify and eliminate biases that could arise in AI systems, ensuring that decisions made by these systems are fair and equitable. Ethical considerations also extend to data privacy, where organizations need to safeguard customer data from misuse and breaches. Adopting ethical AI practices is not only a regulatory requirement but also a pathway to building trust with clients and broader stakeholders.

Finally, as we prepare for an AI-driven future, the overarching objective should remain centered on enhancing value for customers and stakeholders. While AI offers remarkable capabilities, it is not an end unto itself. The success of AI integration in finance will ultimately be measured by the tangible benefits it delivers—be it in the form of improved service delivery, better risk management, more accessible financial products, or heightened transparency. Maintaining a customer-centric focus ensures that AI innovations are aligned with the needs and expectations of the market.

The journey to a transformative future powered by AI in finance is not without its hurdles. Yet, with strategic preparation and thoughtful implementation, the industry stands to gain unprecedented knowledge, efficiency, and innovation. Embracing this future means committing to a vision that balances technological advancement with ethical responsibility, creating a financial ecosystem that is as inclusive as it is advanced.

Chapter 23:
Case Studies in Financial AI

In the dynamic landscape of finance, artificial intelligence is making its mark not only through theoretical advancements but also via practical implementations showcasing its potential and limitations. Let's explore some real-world case studies where AI has been both a disruptor and a solution provider. One fascinating example is the application of AI in predictive analytics to streamline trading operations, leading to significant operational efficiencies and increased returns. However, not all implementations are smooth; some organizations face hurdles like data quality issues and integration challenges that can stymie progress. Through these case studies, finance professionals can glean insights into effective applications of AI, understand common pitfalls, and better evaluate the varying degrees of success and failure in AI-driven projects. It's clear that as the technology matures, continuous learning and adaptation remain key for leveraging AI's full potential.

Real World Applications and Lessons Learned

The case studies presented throughout this book illuminate both the profound and the practical impacts of artificial intelligence in the financial sector. Each real-world example offers a unique glimpse into how different segments of the industry are leveraging AI to enhance efficiency, accuracy, and strategic decision-making. From the bustling floors of stock exchanges to the intricate world of credit scoring, AI's reach extends far and wide. Yet, the journey is marked with lessons that reveal the nuances of technology adoption in a highly regulated and risk-averse environment.

One of the key lessons learned from implementing AI in finance is the importance of data quality and accessibility. The power of AI lies in its ability to analyze vast amounts of data swiftly and accurately. However, the models can only be as good as the data they are trained on. Financial institutions have grappled with legacy systems and disparate data sources that can hinder the efficacy of AI initiatives. Standardizing data practices and investing in robust data management infrastructure has thus become paramount for firms aiming to harness the full potential of AI.

The integration of natural language processing (NLP) in investment research exemplifies AI's capability to transform traditional financial practices. By rapidly parsing through and analyzing news articles, earning reports, and social media feeds, NLP tools provide investors with real-time sentiment analyses, helping them make informed investment decisions. This shift toward AI-enhanced research underscores a larger trend of moving beyond quantitative data to incorporate qualitative insights—a transition that opens new avenues for investment strategies but also challenges existing analytical frameworks.

Fraud detection is another area where AI's application has yielded tangible benefits. Traditional fraud detection methods often involved rule-based systems that were not only labor-intensive but also prone to human error. AI techniques, on the other hand, leverage machine learning models that continuously improve as they are fed new data. These systems can detect anomalous patterns suggesting fraudulent activities more accurately and swiftly than human analysts. However, the deployment of such systems does not come without its hiccups. Companies have learned the hard way that over-reliance on AI without adequate human oversight can lead to false positives or overlooked criminal patterns.

The rise of robo-advisors in wealth management has democratized financial advice, making it accessible to a broader audience. These platforms employ sophisticated algorithms to customize investment portfolios for individual clients, based on their financial goals and risk appetites. However, real-world implementations of robo-advisors have taught companies about the importance of balancing automation with human interaction. Clients still value the reassurance and personalized touch that human advisors provide, especially during volatile market conditions. Thus, successful firms have integrated hybrid models that combine the scalability of AI with human expertise.

Ethical considerations have emerged as a pivotal area of focus as AI becomes more entrenched in financial systems. Instances of bias in AI algorithms, particularly in credit scoring and lending decisions, have highlighted the socio-economic impacts of flawed models. Financial institutions now recognize the necessity of developing transparent and fair AI systems. Ensuring diversity in training data and implementing rigorous bias-detection methodologies are critical steps that stakeholders are integrating into their AI development processes.

Innovations in AI-driven financial forecasting also reflect both the promise and complexity of AI in finance. Predictive models have become invaluable in analyzing market trends and economic indicators. However, the real world often presents variables that are unpredictable and outside the scope of historical data on which AI models are trained. The financial crisis of 2007-2008 serves as a solemn reminder of the unpredictability of market dynamics. Modern AI systems are therefore being designed with enhanced learning techniques that allow them to adapt more efficiently to new patterns, thus improving their predictive accuracy.

As collaboration between startups and established financial institutions grows, the lessons learned have influenced both sides of the partnership. Startups, often more agile and willing to experiment, bring innovative AI solutions to the table, while larger institutions provide resources and market access. Successful collaborations have hinged on clear communication and alignment of goals, demonstrating the importance of fostering a mutually beneficial relationship. However, challenges remain in reconciling the cultural differences and operational scales between nimble startups and traditional, perhaps bureaucratic, financial giants.

Building AI-ready systems has proven essential yet challenging. Financial firms must navigate the difficulties of integrating AI technologies into existing infrastructures. This task requires not just technical upgrades but also a shift in organizational culture towards embracing digital transformation. Lessons from early adopters emphasize the importance of cross-departmental collaboration and continuous employee training programs to facilitate this change. By investing in human capital and fostering a culture of innovation, organizations can overcome resistance to change and successfully integrate AI into their financial operations.

In summary, as AI continues to evolve and integrate deeper into the financial landscape, the real-world applications reveal both opportunities and hurdles. Each lesson serves as a stepping stone towards more refined and responsible AI implementations. Financial institutions are called not only to harness the technological advancements AI offers but also to approach these innovations with a mindset geared towards ethical and efficient utilization. The fusion of technology and human insight remains fundamental to achieving the full potential of AI in finance. These insights, learned through trial and experience, pave the way for a future where AI and finance are inseparably linked, driving forward a new era of financial innovation and resilience.

Evaluating Success and Failures

As we delve into the intricacies of *Case Studies in Financial AI*, understanding the dualistic nature of success and failure is paramount. The financial sector, notorious for its complexities and constant evolution, serves as both a fertile ground and a harsh testing field for AI applications. Evaluating the success stories alongside notable failures offers invaluable insights into what drives innovation forward and what pitfalls to avoid.

Success in AI-driven financial applications often hinges on data accuracy, algorithm robustness, and the prevailing market conditions. Take algorithmic trading, for instance. Companies that have succeeded have done so by harnessing large datasets, creating sophisticated models capable of real-time learning, and adapting swiftly to market fluctuations. These firms typically have a competitive edge due to their technological infrastructure, deep financial knowledge, and adept handling of regulatory frameworks. However, it's not just the technical capabilities that determine success; strategic vision and organizational buy-in are crucial. When leadership understands the potential and limitations of AI, adoption becomes holistic, fostering environments where AI solutions can thrive.

Failures, on the other hand, often spring from an overreliance on technology without a clear understanding of the underlying financial principles. Some initiatives have collapsed simply because they failed to incorporate essential financial know-how into their AI models. In some cases, practitioners overestimated AI's predictive capabilities in scenarios where historical data wasn't a reliable predictor of future events. These failures serve as a stark reminder of the need for balance between technological innovation and traditional financial wisdom.

Consider the phenomenon of high-frequency trading (HFT). Although AI has the potential to revolutionize HFT, some ventures have faltered due to unforeseen variables such as latency issues and network failures. Additionally, trading environments are impacted by external factors like geopolitical events or sudden regulatory changes, which AI models might not anticipate. Rigidity in model design can prevent necessary recalibrations, leading to financial losses. Hence, success is often synonymous with the flexibility and adaptability of AI models in accommodating new data or shifts in market paradigms.

Moving into the domain of credit scoring, we observe a different kind of learning curve. AI's prowess in predictive analytics has improved credit risk assessments, but its journey has been marred by ethical and bias-related controversies. Companies that achieved success aligned their models with ethical AI practices, ensuring transparency and fairness. Conversely, those failing in this sphere typically ignored the biases ingrained within their data, leading to discriminatory practices. Evaluating these cases underscores the necessity for rigorous bias mitigation strategies before deploying AI on sensitive financial tasks.

Robo-advisors have also experienced mixed outcomes in wealth management. Successful deployments cater to a wide array of investor needs, offering personalized investment strategies based on comprehensive data analysis and individual risk tolerance. However, when customer experience is neglected, or the AI's recommendations aren't clearly communicated, dissatisfaction and withdrawal are likely. Balancing AI-driven insights with human touchpoints can often spell the difference between a thriving service and a lackluster one.

While AI in fraud detection has made significant strides, failures often emerge from an inability to keep pace with the rapidly evolving methods of fraudsters. The technology's response must be as dynamic and resourceful as the threats it encounters. Successful systems incorporate machine learning capabilities that learn and adapt, continuously improving their detection mechanisms. Static systems, however, become obsolete quickly, highlighting the consequences of resting on initial successes without continued innovation.

The unpredictable nature of financial markets adds another layer of complexity to implementing AI solutions, manifesting in unpredictable successes and failures. The success in venture capital investments, for instance, owes much to AI's data-crunching power to unearth lucrative opportunities by analyzing market trends and consumer data. However, ventures that ignored market sentiments or relied excessively on quantitative analysis without qualitative insights often stumbled. These outcomes showcase the criticality of a hybrid approach in AI applications—leveraging data science and human intuition symbiotically.

Another axis of evaluation is regulatory compliance, which acts as a double-edged sword. On one hand, innovations propelled by AI have facilitated adherence to complex regulatory requirements through automation and predictive analytics. On the other, failures arise from misjudging regulatory thresholds or underestimating compliance complexities. Companies neglecting this facet not only face punitive action but also incur reputational damage, displaying that compliance and innovation must evolve together.

The assessment of successes and failures in AI in finance thus calls for a holistic view—a deep dive into both the quantitative metrics of success such as ROI and market share, and the qualitative elements like customer satisfaction and ethical considerations. For investors and tech enthusiasts keen on financial disruption, these case studies provide blueprints and cautionary tales, emphasizing the importance of constant learning and adaptation.

Lastly, the cultural aspect shouldn't be overlooked. Organizational culture significantly influences both the adoption and the success of

AI initiatives. Firms fostering a culture of innovation and agility are generally the ones benefiting most from AI, while those adversarial to change typically lag. Emphasizing learning and adaptability can bridge the gap between potential failures and remarkable successes.

In conclusion, the varied landscapes of successes and failures in financial AI are decorated with lessons for future endeavors. Striking the right balance between innovative zeal and cautious pragmatism, understanding both data and human narratives, can pave the way for prosperous engagement with financial AI advancements.

Chapter 24:
AI and Sustainable Finance

In the rapidly evolving world of finance, AI stands at the forefront of a transformative wave, reshaping how institutions approach sustainable finance. The incorporation of AI technologies in managing Environmental, Social, and Governance (ESG) investments not only optimizes returns but also enhances transparency and accountability, crucial factors for investors who prioritize sustainability. Advanced machine learning algorithms analyze a myriad of data points—from carbon emissions to corporate social initiatives—helping investors identify opportunities and risks with precision previously unattainable. Moreover, AI's ability to process vast datasets enables real-time assessments of sustainability impacts, allowing stakeholders to make informed, ethical investment decisions. This synergy between AI and sustainable finance holds the potential to influence capital allocation globally, encouraging businesses to adopt more sustainable practices and ultimately foster a resilient, ethical financial ecosystem. By leveraging AI, finance professionals can pioneer a future where economic growth aligns harmoniously with environmental stewardship and social responsibility.

Promoting Sustainability through AI

In the rapidly evolving landscape of finance, integrating artificial intelligence with sustainability initiatives presents both challenges and opportunities. As global awareness of environmental issues grows, so does the pressure on industries to adopt sustainable practices. For the financial sector, leveraging AI's capabilities in promoting sustainability is not just a trend but a necessity. AI, with its unparalleled ability to process vast amounts of data and glean insights, is poised to play a pivotal role in steering the finance industry towards sustainable practices.

AI has the potential to revolutionize how data related to sustainability is analyzed and utilized. By employing machine learning algorithms, financial institutions can better assess the sustainability credentials of investments and projects. This is particularly useful for evaluating the environmental impact and carbon footprint of industries, helping investors make informed decisions aligned with their ethical standards. Such assessments not only streamline the decision-making process but also enhance transparency and accountability among corporates.

Climate change and sustainability risks are complex, requiring advanced tools to decode and address them effectively. Here, AI can assist by enabling predictive analytics and scenario modeling. Financial institutions can simulate various climate scenarios and their potential impacts on investments. This allows firms to prepare and adapt to forthcoming environmental regulations, market shifts, and consumer preferences. AI-driven predictive models can offer financial institutions a competitive edge by identifying long-term, sustainable opportunities that others might overlook.

Supply chains, a key area affecting sustainability, benefit significantly from AI integration. Transparent supply chain practices have become increasingly vital for companies committed to environmental and social governance (ESG) criteria. AI systems can enhance supply chain visibility, tracing the journey of raw materials from sourcing to final product delivery. This capability helps in detecting inefficiencies, minimizing waste, and ensuring compliance with sustainability standards across borders. As a result, companies are better positioned to make decisions that align with sustainable development goals.

Beyond operational efficiencies, AI can facilitate more sustainable financial practices through smart contract solutions. Utilizing blockchain technology, AI can foster trust in sustainable finance by executing contracts automatically when predefined sustainability conditions are met. This automation reduces the need for manual oversight and ensures that all parties comply with ESG criteria. It enhances credibility in green finance projects, potentially increasing investment in renewable energy sources and sustainable infrastructure.

The integration of AI in sustainable finance also impacts the consumer side of the equation. Personal finance applications that incorporate AI can guide users to invest in ethically sound funds by providing recommendations based on individual preferences and predefined ESG metrics. These tools empower consumers to contribute to sustainability through their investment choices, promoting broader societal shifts towards environmentally friendly practices.

While the potential benefits of AI in promoting sustainability are significant, challenges must be addressed. The first hurdle is the availability and reliability of data. AI algorithms rely heavily on high-quality data to make accurate predictions and assessments. Financial institutions must prioritize data collection and management practices, ensuring the information used is accurate, comprehensive, and up-to-date. Additionally, ensuring data privacy and security remains a top concern, especially when dealing with sensitive environmental metrics.

Another consideration is the ethical dimension of AI deployment in sustainable finance. As AI systems gain autonomy, questions around bias, accountability, and transparency become more pronounced. Financial institutions must develop frameworks to ensure AI systems operate ethically while minimizing unintended biases against certain stakeholders or geographies. Building AI systems that not only enhance financial returns but also foster sustainability will require cross-sector collaboration, involving experts from finance, technology, and environmental science.

The intersection of AI and sustainability in finance also hinges on regulatory support. Policymakers must establish clear guidelines that encourage sustainable investments while fostering innovation in AI applications. Such regulations can incentivize financial institutions to adopt AI-driven sustainable practices while mitigating risks associated with lax oversight and potential exploitation.

Finally, financial institutions need to foster a culture of continuous learning and adaptation. As AI technologies evolve, so too will their applications in sustainability. Institutions that remain agile, investing in employee education and development, will be best positioned to harness AI's full potential in promoting sustainability.

In conclusion, the journey towards sustainability in finance is complex but promising, with AI as a critical enabler of change. As financial institutions embrace AI to enhance sustainable practices, they will not only contribute to a greener future but also uncover lucrative opportunities that benefit stakeholders and the planet alike. The fusion of AI and sustainability holds the promise of a transformative impact on the financial sector, aligning economic goals with ecological imperatives.

AI in Environmental, Social, and Governance (ESG) Investment

As the financial industry continues to witness an unprecedented transformation, the integration of artificial intelligence (AI) within Environmental, Social, and Governance (ESG) investment emerges as a pivotal trend. Traditionally viewed as an essential framework for sustainable investing, ESG criteria help investors identify companies with ethical practices across environmental stewardship, social responsibility, and corporate governance. However, assessing these criteria can be labor-intensive and subjective. Here, AI steps in as a game-changer, offering enhanced capabilities to scrutinize and analyze vast datasets, thus revolutionizing ESG investment methodologies.

The surge in demand for ESG-centric portfolios reflects a broader societal shift towards sustainability and ethical governance. Investors are keen to align their financial objectives with these values but face challenges in accurately evaluating companies' ESG strengths. AI enables the assimilation and analysis of large volumes of structured and unstructured data from diverse sources, such as environmental reports, social media, regulatory filings, and more. These AI-driven analyses provide a more nuanced understanding of a company's ESG performance, facilitating well-informed investment decisions.

One of the key areas where AI makes significant strides is in environmental analysis. AI algorithms can monitor corporate carbon footprints, track renewable energy usage, and evaluate waste management practices with a level of precision and efficiency unattainable through traditional methods. For instance, satellite imagery enhanced by machine learning models can assess deforestation levels or monitor industrial pollution in real-time, providing investors with granular insights into a company's environmental impact. This real-time analysis is invaluable for investors seeking to support companies that are leaders in environmental sustainability.

On the social front, AI assists investors in evaluating labor practices, product safety records, and community engagement efforts. Natural language processing (NLP) technologies parse through extensive reports and public records, identifying language that indicates potential social risks or strengths. By analyzing sentiment from news articles, social media, and employee reviews, AI helps investors gauge employee satisfaction and public perception, which are indicative of a company's social responsibility and retention capabilities.

In terms of governance, AI facilitates meticulous scrutiny of corporate practices, management behaviors, and board compositions. Using machine learning models, investors can identify patterns that suggest potential red flags, such as conflicts of interest, unethical board behavior, or poor managerial practices. Moreover, AI can track shifts in corporate governance structures, such as transparency in executive compensation or shareholder voting policies, empowering investors to make governance-focused investment choices.

Despite the apparent benefits, integrating AI into ESG investment processes isn't without its challenges. Data quality and availability remain significant issues. Many companies still lack comprehensive ESG reporting, leading to potential biases in AI analyses. Furthermore, the inherent complexity and multifaceted nature of ESG criteria might present difficulties in algorithmic interpretation, demanding continual refinement and training of AI systems to improve accuracy and reliability.

The potential of AI in ESG investing transcends mere risk assessment; it also brings new opportunities for identifying value in untapped markets. By uncovering emergent trends and predicting future ESG performance, AI helps investors craft proactive strategies, capitalizing on shifts towards sustainable business models and practices. As AI progresses, its role in ESG investment will likely expand, offering unprecedented insights and shaping the sustainable finance landscape.

There's a growing collaborative effort between fintech startups and established financial institutions to innovate in AI-driven ESG analysis tools. These partnerships are crucial in developing sophisticated, user-friendly platforms that enable both institutional and retail investors to integrate ESG factors into their portfolios effectively. The symbiotic relationship between AI innovation and ESG investment not only enhances portfolio performance but also contributes to a broader societal impact by fostering responsible corporate behavior.

The regulatory environment also plays a fundamental role in shaping the adoption and integration of AI in ESG analysis. With governments and regulatory bodies increasingly emphasizing sustainable finance, there's a push towards greater disclosure and standardization in ESG reporting. This regulatory shift not only aids in the better functioning of AI models by providing richer data sets but also aligns investment strategies with global sustainability goals.

Looking forward, the fusion of AI with ESG investment paradigms is set to create more dynamic and responsive financial markets, where sustainability isn't just a checkbox but a core component of financial strategies. As AI technologies continue to evolve, their application in ESG investment will not only enhance the transparency and accountability of corporate practices but also pave the way for a more sustainable, responsible financial system.

In conclusion, the integration of AI into ESG investing represents a transformative movement within the financial sector. By leveraging AI's capabilities in data analysis, monitoring, and predictive modeling, investors are better equipped to make informed decisions that not only yield financial returns but also contribute to the creation of a more sustainable and equitable future. As the appetite for ESG investments grows, so does AI's potential to redefine the standards for ethical and responsible investing, reshaping the very fabric of modern finance.

Chapter 25:
Developing Skills for AI in Finance

As artificial intelligence reshapes the financial sector, cultivating the right skill set becomes essential for professionals eager to stay abreast of this transformation. At the intersection of finance and technology, individuals must develop a diverse array of skills that bridges both domains. Mastery in data science, programming languages like Python, and comprehension of machine learning models is increasingly indispensable. Moreover, understanding how these technologies integrate into financial processes, such as algorithmic trading and risk management, equips finance experts with unparalleled versatility. Beyond technical prowess, the ability to interpret complex data insights for strategic decision-making positions professionals to capitalize on AI-driven innovations. Educational resources proliferate, ranging from online courses to bootcamps, offering opportunities to hone these critical skills. Ultimately, it's this blend of finance acumen and technical expertise that will empower practitioners to navigate and lead in an AI-enhanced financial landscape.

Skills Needed for the AI-Finance Landscape

The fusion of artificial intelligence (AI) within the financial industry is transforming traditional financial practices, making it crucial for professionals to acquire a new set of skills. Understanding AI's implications requires a blend of competencies that intersect both financial acumen and technological expertise. This landscape is not just about being able to program or analyze data but also about comprehending regulatory environments, ethical implications, and the strategic use of AI in decision-making.

First and foremost, professionals in this domain need a robust understanding of data analytics. Financial markets generate massive amounts of data, and those who can effectively harness and interpret this data are invaluable. Skills like data warehousing, data mining, and proficiency in data visualization tools such as Tableau or Power BI are essential. Being able to transform raw data into actionable insights can significantly impact investment strategies and risk management processes.

Equally important is the knowledge of machine learning (ML) algorithms. Understanding both supervised and unsupervised learning methods is crucial, as is familiarity with tools and languages such as Python, R, TensorFlow, and Keras. These tools are at the core of developing predictive models that can automate decision-making in trading, credit scoring, and beyond. The ability to design and fine-tune these algorithms to adapt to ever-changing market conditions is a key asset.

Moreover, the ability to work with natural language processing (NLP) tools is increasingly valuable. Financial markets are influenced not just by numeric data but also by reports, news, and social media sentiment. Skills in text analysis and sentiment analysis tools can help derive insights from these diverse sources. Knowing how to leverage APIs like those from Google Cloud Natural Language or IBM Watson can offer a competitive edge in understanding market dynamics.

In addition to technical skills, financial professionals must develop an understanding of blockchain technology. Blockchain's intersection with AI can enhance transparency, security, and efficiency in financial transactions. Knowledge of how distributed ledgers work, and familiarity with platforms like Ethereum or Hyperledger, can be critical for those involved in areas such as asset management or fraud detection.

With the increasing integration of AI, cybersecurity skills are also indispensable. Protecting sensitive financial data from cyber threats is of paramount importance. Skills in cybersecurity measures specifically tailored to integrate with AI technologies, such as anomaly detection systems and AI-driven encryption, are becoming standard requirements. Understanding cybersecurity protocols and best practices reduces risk and ensures the integrity of financial systems.

Professionals need to also cultivate an understanding of ethical considerations involved in the implementation of AI in finance. This includes navigating the complexities of regulatory requirements and ensuring compliance. Familiarity with laws like GDPR for data protection and knowledge of future regulatory frameworks impacting AI's use in finance will be advantageous. An ethical mindset ensures AI systems are not only legal but also fair and equitable.

Strategic thinking skills are necessary to maximize AI's value in finance. This involves not only the technical execution of AI projects but also aligning them with business objectives. Professionals need to assess how AI can solve specific financial challenges and generate value, whether it's through cost reduction, enhanced decision-making, or improved customer satisfaction. Skills in project management and strategic planning are vital for successful AI implementation.

Communication and collaboration skills should not be overlooked. Working in AI-finance often requires interdisciplinary collaboration. Communicating complex technical concepts to stakeholders who may not be technically inclined, and translating these into actionable strategies is crucial. Additionally, collaborative projects that require teams across data science, compliance, and financial analysis necessitate strong interpersonal skills.

Finally, a dedication to lifelong learning is essential. AI is a rapidly evolving field, and staying updated with the latest advancements, tools, and practices is crucial for anyone in the AI-finance landscape. Engaging in continued education, whether through online courses, workshops, or industry conferences, ensures that skills remain sharp and relevant. This commitment to growth helps professionals anticipate future trends and prepare for advancements that could shape the finance industry.

In essence, thriving in the AI-finance landscape means embracing a multidisciplinary skill set. It's not enough to be a financial expert or a tech enthusiast in isolation; the future belongs to those who can blend these areas seamlessly. As AI continues to evolve, so too must the professionals who operate within its sphere, positioning themselves not just as passive users of technology, but as proactive drivers of innovation.

Education and Training Resources

To thrive in the rapidly evolving landscape of AI in finance, professionals need access to robust education and training resources. As AI technologies become more ingrained in financial operations, the demand for skilled professionals who can harness these tools effectively is on the rise. Fortunately, a wide array of resources is available to guide those striving to develop these crucial skills.

Universities worldwide have recognized the burgeoning need for coursework tailored to AI applications in finance. Many prestigious institutions now offer specialized master's programs and electives focused on financial technology. These programs often blend traditional finance studies with advanced modules on machine learning, data science, and algorithmic trading. The University of California, Berkeley, and the Massachusetts Institute of Technology are just a couple of examples where such integrative learning environments flourish. These programs typically include hands-on projects that simulate real-world financial scenarios, providing students with practical experience.

In addition to formal education, online platforms have democratized access to AI and finance training. Websites like Coursera, edX, and Udacity offer comprehensive courses designed by industry experts and often in partnership with leading universities. These platforms cater to a range of learners, from beginners looking to dip their toes into AI basics, to advanced practitioners searching for niche specializations. Participants can often engage in these courses at their own pace, making it easier for working professionals to balance continuous learning with their careers.

Aside from structured courses, curated content from industry conferences and workshops can play a significant role in education as well. These events are often organized by financial institutions, tech companies, or academic bodies aiming to showcase cutting-edge AI innovations. Conferences such as the AI in Finance Summit provide attendees with a chance to learn directly from pioneers in the field, gaining insights that textbooks might not yet capture. Networking at these events can also lead to mentorship opportunities and collaborative projects, further enriching the learning experience.

Continuing professional development is important, and certifications are another viable path to gaining recognition for AI proficiency in finance. Organizations like the CFA Institute have started offering certificates that focus specifically on AI and machine learning skills, addressing the nuanced needs of finance professionals. These certifications not only enhance a resume but also ensure professionals remain competitive in a field where technological expertise is increasingly pivotal.

Self-study remains a critical component for skill development in this arena. With the plethora of available books, research papers, and online forums, individuals can take charge of their learning. Titles like "Artificial Intelligence: A Guide to Intelligent Systems" and research papers published in journals such as the Journal of Finance or the AI & Society journal offer deep dives into specific subject matter. Online communities, including Stack Overflow and Reddit, provide platforms where enthusiasts can exchange ideas, solve problems collaboratively, and stay abreast of emerging trends.

For those more inclined towards a practice-oriented approach, AI-focused hackathons provide immersive learning experiences. Events like these are organized by tech companies and universities to push the boundaries of innovation in real time. They often pose complex financial dilemmas requiring innovative AI solutions, challenging participants to apply their theoretical knowledge practically. Over time, such experiences help refine skills that are directly applicable in financial workplaces.

Moreover, mentorship and peer learning should not be underestimated. Engaging with those who have hands-on experience in utilizing AI within financial institutions can provide invaluable insights. Many finance professionals are turning to LinkedIn and other professional networks to find mentors who can provide guidance tailored to their career paths and ambitions. Peer learning groups, often organized within workplaces or educational settings, foster environments of shared knowledge and experience exchange, which can enhance understanding and retention of complex concepts.

For professionals working in the finance sector, keeping pace with the changes in AI technology necessitates a commitment to lifelong learning. Corporate training programs are an essential resource to stay updated with the latest tools and methodologies. Organizations investing in such training programs signify a commitment to maintaining a competitive edge by equipping their employees with the necessary skills to leverage AI effectively. These programs are tailored to the specific needs and strategies of the company, ensuring relevancy to the current business environment.

In summary, a multifaceted approach combining formal education, online learning, certification programs, self-study, practical applications, and mentorship offers a comprehensive strategy for developing the skills needed to navigate the AI-finance landscape. As AI continues to transform the financial industry, professionals who engage with these diverse education and training resources are well-positioned to not only adapt but lead in this transformative era. Through dedication and consistent effort, acquiring expertise in AI can open up new avenues for innovation and career advancement in finance.

Conclusion

The transformative power of artificial intelligence in the financial industry is nothing short of profound. As we've ventured through this book, we've explored various facets of AI application in finance, from algorithmic trading and robo-advisors to risk management and fraud detection. Each chapter has unveiled a layer of what AI can achieve, reflecting a future that is both exciting and challenging.

In this rapidly evolving landscape, AI is a catalyst for change, pushing boundaries beyond traditional finance practices. It's not just about doing things faster or cheaper—it's about doing things better. The potential of AI to enhance decision-making processes, identify patterns often invisible to the human eye, and drive efficiency stands as a testament to its revolutionary capabilities. As AI technologies continue to mature, financial institutions are likely to experience shifts that redefine their operations and market strategies.

However, one can't overlook the importance of ethical considerations and regulatory frameworks that accompany such innovations. Throughout our analysis, the necessity for balancing progress with responsibility has been a recurring theme. As AI tools become more intricate and widely adopted, ensuring that systems are fair, transparent, and accountable remains crucial. This balance will be pivotal in fostering trust among consumers and investors, who must feel confident that their data and interests are safeguarded.

Looking ahead, the role of AI in sustainable finance will most likely gain greater prominence. As the world grapples with climate change and socio-economic inequities, AI holds the promise of driving sustainability initiatives and improving ESG investment strategies. The intersection of technology and sustainable finance could usher in new opportunities for creating value aligned with societal goals.

Moreover, the global impact of AI further highlights the diversity of its applications across market contexts. We've seen how AI adoption varies globally, influenced by cultural, economic, and regulatory factors. This variation poses both challenges and opportunities for fostering international collaborations and opening new markets for financial innovations.

Education and skill development are key enablers of this AI-driven transformation. As financial professionals and tech enthusiasts venture into this evolving landscape, equipping themselves with the right skills will be vital. Whether it's understanding complex algorithms or navigating regulatory requirements, the knowledge landscape is ever-expanding.

In conclusion, the journey of AI in finance is still unfolding. While much progress has been made, the horizon is filled with potential developments. Stakeholders across the financial industry must be prepared to adapt and embrace the changes AI brings. By doing so, they will not only stay competitive but also contribute to shaping a financial ecosystem that is innovative, inclusive, and resilient. The future of finance is not just about surviving but thriving in this new AI era, with the opportunity to redefine what is possible. As we step forward, the relentless march of innovation paired with thoughtful consideration of its impacts will be our guiding light.

Appendix A:
Appendix

In any comprehensive exploration of artificial intelligence (AI) in finance, it's essential to compile additional insights, resources, and tools that can further illuminate the subject. This appendix serves as a crucial addendum, providing supplementary information that complements the main content of this book. Here, we delve into various aspects not extensively covered in the preceding chapters, offering a detailed examination designed to enrich the reader's understanding of AI's transformative role in the financial industry.

Further Resources

Books and Academic Journals: Dive deeper into AI and finance by consulting academic journals and seminal books. Titles such as "Machine Learning for Asset Managers" and "AI in Finance: A Strategic Guide for Business Leaders" offer further reading into how AI strategies can be effectively implemented in financial contexts.

Online Courses and Certifications: Numerous platforms provide courses focused on AI applications in finance. Websites like Coursera, edX, and Udacity offer a range of programs from introductory to advanced levels, enabling finance professionals to build or enhance their AI-related competencies.

Industry Tools and Software

Various tools have emerged to cater to the growing demand for AI-driven solutions in finance. Below are some notable mentions:

AI-Driven Trading Platforms: These platforms leverage machine learning algorithms to offer automated trading solutions, helping traders execute strategies with precision and speed.

Risk Management Software: Utilize state-of-the-art predictive analytics to identify potential risks, allowing firms to make informed decisions and adjust strategies proactively.

Glossary of Terms

Understanding technical terms is vital when navigating the intersection of AI and finance. Here's a brief glossary of essential terms:

Quantitative Analysis: The use of mathematical and statistical modeling to understand financial trends and make investment decisions.

Sentiment Analysis: A technique used to determine the tone of textual data, which is particularly useful in analyzing market sentiment based on news articles or social media.

Robustness: Refers to an AI model's ability to maintain its performance when faced with real-world data outside its training set.

Conclusion

As the financial industry continues to evolve with technological advancements, staying updated and well-informed is crucial for anyone engaged in the field. This appendix, while supplementary, plays a significant role in equipping readers with the necessary tools, resources, and knowledge, ultimately providing a broadened perspective on AI's profound impact in finance. We hope these resources will be a valuable part of your ongoing exploration into the future of finance.

www.ingramcontent.com/pod-product-compliance
Lightning Source LLC
Chambersburg PA
CBHW051238050326
40689CB00007B/966